Mary Lou –

Keep up the

Climb!!. The view from the

summit is amazing!

Peace

Mike

CHOOSING HIGHER GROUND

CHOOSING HIGHER GROUND

WORKING AND LIVING IN THE VALUES ECONOMY

MICHAEL WEISMAN

with Beth Jusino

NORTIA
PRESS

www.nortiapress.com

2321 E 4th Street, C-219
Santa Ana, CA 92705
contact @ nortiapress.com

Choosing higher ground. Working and living in the values economy.

ISBN: 978-1-940503-15-8
Library of Congress Control Number: 2016909260

Printed in the United States of America

How to get the best of it all? One must conquer, achieve, get to the top; one must know the end to be convinced that one can win the end - to know there's no dream that mustn't be dared. . . Is this the summit, crowning the day? How cool and quiet! We're not exultant; but delighted, joyful; soberly astonished. . . Have we vanquished an enemy? None but ourselves. Have we gained success? That word means nothing here. Have we won a kingdom? No. . . and yes. We have achieved an ultimate satisfaction. . . fulfilled a destiny. . . To struggle and to understand—never this last without the other; such is the law. . .

—George Mallory, *Climbing Everest: The Complete Writings of George Mallory*

To Chesley

IT'S NOT WORKING ANYMORE

Growing up in the 1950s, my TV hero was Darren Stephens of *Bewitched*. That probably explains why I chose a career in advertising. For almost four decades, I've wooed clients, hired employees, welcomed and said goodbye to partners, struggled through economic slumps, and celebrated victories.

Not surprisingly, it wasn't as simple as it looked on TV. The business world I glimpsed in thirty-minute stories is drastically different than where we live and work today, and there were days when I really doubted that this was all worth it.

Perhaps you've felt that way, too.

In the United States, we give more hours to our jobs in the average week than to any other single part of our lives, including sleep. The daily responsibilities, trials, and satisfactions of managing a business or career require an enormous investment of energy. Smart phones keep us tied to work twenty-four hours a day—a reality I was reminded of at ten o'clock last night when I checked my email "one last time" and saw that one of our senior account executives was still at it, corresponding with a nervous client about a

1

presentation the next morning.

What do we get in return for that kind of commitment? For too many leaders today, the answer is "not enough."

Work has taken up more and more of our lives, but it hasn't made our lives better. When I talk to my seemingly-successful colleagues, clients, and friends about their experiences, instead of satisfaction they often share a deep sense of exhaustion. In fact, for most leaders who have been at this for a few years—or, like me, a few decades—the long hours of meetings, spreadsheets, and office politics have taken their toll. Projects and products that once excited us now seem flat, even as we acquire more and increase revenue.

It's not just executives and senior leaders who report feeling this way. Everyone from CEOs to interns to customers seems tired of business as usual. As we step, tentatively, out of the Great Recession, there's a lingering air of weariness and a culture of suspicion. The once-solid future is now shaky. The outcomes are no longer assured.

Does this sound familiar?

Wherever you fall on your organizational chart, *Choosing Higher Ground* is my message of hope for you. On the pages that follow I'll show you how I learned, with the help of some smart and honest people, how to think about doing business in a whole new way. We're going to explore, in depth, what it means for you and your business to enter the Values Economy. Using some of the best social science research available, and case studies from companies both large and small, I'll show you how defining and working toward a set of shared values can change your culture, motivate your employees, inspire your customers, help you survive a crisis—and help your bottom line. Most importantly, I hope to paint a vivid picture of how good it will feel and how much it can change for you, personally, to live in the Values Economy.

This isn't a "get rich quick" guide, although there is a direct correlation between values-driven leadership and revenue growth. And it's not a warm-and-fuzzy book that tells you to think positive thoughts to find success. There's a lot of hard work for you to do, and I'm going to show you, step by step, how to do it. Changing a culture takes time, earning trust takes time, and time is a precious commodity for most businesses today. But as we'll see, with recent culture shifts it's not an option anymore; it's a necessity.

Together we'll unpack the opportunities of the workplace, and I'll give you practical, field-tested techniques that will help you change yourself and your business in order to thrive in an economy that continues to shift under our feet.

I want to be clear: this isn't just a message for executives and CEOs. Whatever your title is, you have a sphere of influence. Every single one of us has a choice about the way that we work and the way we live. Every single one of us makes decisions that ripple out farther than you probably realize. While this is primarily a book about changing business, the Values Economy can change the way you see yourself and the people around you. It certainly has for me, and I'll tell you more of my own story as we go.

But first, let me tell you about Joe.

"I'M AFRAID OF DYING"

I'd just finished my standard pitch to a prospective new client—a mid-sized national chain of self-storage units.* I didn't feel like it had gone that well; the

---

* Throughout this book, I'll tell you a number of stories about specific clients and friends. Whenever possible, I'll use real names. But sometimes, to preserve their privacy, I need to change identifying details. This is understandably one of those cases.

Chief Marketing Officer had been polite, but not enthusiastic. When I was done she thanked me, said they'd be in touch, and everyone booked for the door. But as I was gathering my things to leave, the CEO, a man named Joe who'd sat quietly in the back of the room while I talked, stepped over and asked if I could chat in his office for a few minutes.

He told his assistant he didn't want to be disturbed, shut the door behind us, and looked me in the eyes.

"Mike, I'm afraid of dying."

Wow, that wasn't the conversation I thought we were going to have.

"Are you telling me you're dying?"

"No, I'm fine." But Joe wasn't fine. He leaned back into his chair and shook his head. "But I'll eventually die. And my company...Mike, I listened to what you said in there, about having a purpose. And all I could think was that we don't have that. It's a serious problem. I built this company from a single empty lot in a bad part of town. I've put everything I have into it, but it's a mess. If I died today, my business would be in shambles."

Joe went on to tell me his story. For twenty years, the company had grown rapidly, even during the recession. In fact, maybe it had grown too rapidly. With a knack for real estate, Joe spent most of his time launching new storage sites, quickly overwhelming his small, family-run office staff's ability to keep up. So five years ago, they'd launched a major reorganization. Joe brought in half a dozen experienced executives and gave them free reign. They changed systems to make them scalable and cleaned up the accounting backlog. They launched a company-wide evaluation of site managers and vendors, and instituted consistent, non-negotiable contracts for tenants. On the surface, the company was thriving, and had even been named one of

4

the state's most promising regional employers. But fixing the administrative process had uncovered other issues.

"The air around here is toxic," he said. "Even I can feel it. Our employees used to invite us to their kids' birthday parties. Now the only time I hear from them is when they complain about not getting enough help, or about being micromanaged. And the new guys here in the office seem to bicker all the time. One of my very first tenants cornered me last week and accused me of getting greedy. I don't want to be remembered for a legacy like that." With a shake of his head, Joe confessed that morale was terrible, employee retention was plummeting, and despite all of the new systems revenue was falling for the first time in their history.

"I'm the CEO, but they don't trust me anymore. I need help."

Joe's situation, unfortunately, wasn't unique. Because of the work I do through The Values Institute—the nonprofit think tank that I run alongside our traditional advertising agency—I've talked to dozens of CEOs and executives who are all facing one form or another of this same crisis.

The first thing we needed to do, I told him, was to find out what was really going on. Plenty of businesses struggle with issues of customer and employee trust, but no two stories are exactly alike.

Using a tool we call the TrustPulse™ survey and a lot of face-to-face interviews, my team collected the honest perspectives of every one of the company's two hundred employees, from Joe himself to the site managers, and even a sampling of their customers. The results were devastating. Joe was right: his focus on growth had happened at the expense of his existing employees. His long-time staff didn't trust him, and his new management team didn't respect each other. There was a huge divide between the executives, who prioritized efficiency and consistency, and the site managers, who worked with the variable needs and quirks of the tenants. The layers of conflict were spilling over to the customers.

Over and over, we heard the same phrases:

This company used to stand for respect and customer service, but not anymore.

I don't know why I come to work every day. I don't know what my role here is.

Customers complain that all we're interested in is their money, and I think they're right.

The management used to bend over backwards for me, but now I'm just a number on a spreadsheet.

I'm looking to change my job to somewhere that values me.

The leaders here are cold, only interested in building more and getting bigger.

Business was booming, but at what cost?

The interviews left my team drained. *Dysfunctional* didn't seem like a strong enough word to describe what we saw. No one seemed to want to be there. I had to swallow my own embarrassment as I walked into their conference room to share the survey results with the executive team.

When I was done talking, the silence stretched for what felt like ten minutes. Finally, one man at the end of the table spoke up.

"We didn't need a survey to tell us that our employees are a bunch of whiners. We're making money, but they just won't get on board."

"It's not the site managers," snapped the woman across from him. "I've been telling you that the finance team is screwing everything up with all their busywork." She added a pointed glare at someone else sitting down the table, presumably the VP in charge of accounting. "But no one at this table wants to talk about it."

This went on for a while, with everyone defending, attacking, and ignoring, all at the same time. At one point, I actually thought that one man was going to cry. This level of frustration was uncharted territory for me.

And then, finally, one of the older men near the head of the table slapped his hand on the table and said, "You know what? This is broken. Look at us. We all feel it, and we all know it's getting worse. I'm tired of it all, and I don't want to do this anymore."

That shut everyone up. In the silence, no one made eye contact.

The company had reached its decision point—in the next five minutes either they would decide to make a change, or they would continue down the same unfulfilling path. I let them sit with that knowledge, and then tried a different, more direct approach. Nodding at the last man who spoke, I said, "He's right. You're a ship that's taking on water fast. But it doesn't have to be that way. There's a way out, but it's going to take a commitment from each of you leaders to keep an open mind, and to do the work. Are you willing to do what it takes to fix this?"

One man shrugged. "Eh" was all he could offer. (He was gone within three months.)

The rest of them nodded, slowly at first. Yes, they wanted the opportunity to change.

The defensive feeling in the room started to fade, just a little.

Joe's staff didn't yet know what I was asking from them, but it was a place to start.

IS THIS ALL THERE IS?

"I'm tired of it all…" said the executive who was watching it all fall apart.

So are many of you.

So was I.

About fifteen years ago, my job didn't feel like it fit as well as it used to. I'd spent almost thirty years in advertising already, most of it running my own agency. I loved being creative. I was proud of the work that we did, branding and bringing expression to hundreds of companies. But the euphoria was fading. Instead of the sense of being on a roller coaster every time we took on a new project, hurtling forward at adrenaline-raising speeds, I was starting to feel like I was on a carousel, spinning in circles and going nowhere.

On the surface, things seemed fine. We were thriving despite the recession. I had fantastic partners, a dedicated staff, and good clients. But in the wake of the emotional turmoil of 9-11, I was starting to see that what I built was fleeting, and that bothered me.

Advertising work is episodic: a client comes in with a product or service and says, "Here's our issue. We need an advertising campaign to fix it." Our team delivers a solution, and the company generally sees a sales spike. They reward us with adulation. But then, three or four months later, the spike settles and the attitude becomes, "what have you done for me lately?"

The people we worked with weren't lasting, either. There was a figure tossed around a lot in the mid-2000s which said that the average marketing executive only lasted eighteen months. I never found the study that confirmed that, but based on my own experience it seemed accurate. Companies wanted a quick fix and a shot of revenue, and if it didn't happen they needed a scapegoat to sacrifice in order to calm nervous investors and curious media.

New CMOs often brought in a new staff, and a new favorite ad agency. We'd be shown the door just as enthusiastically as we were invited in, and they'd hire a new agency for a different quick fix.

We were like the toddler who builds a tower of five or six blocks, and then in her excitement knocks it down and has to start over.

Consumer-facing businesses treated advertising like the secret sauce to success. We were held accountable for a company's short-term success, even though our agency didn't control anything that happened beyond the campaign, like the sales process, the front-line staff, or the customers' actual experiences. Too often, we would bring them into the door of a local restaurant, only for the service to be disappointing. Or they might buy a product because of a message we wrote, but the quality of the product itself didn't live up to the promise.

When I stepped away from my own ego (*What we're doing is brilliant! It will change everything!*), I started to realize that the approach didn't make sense. There was a lot more to the way an organization functioned than its ad campaign. So why was all the pressure on us? Why would a business bypass their own people and treat some billboards and a TV commercial as the Holy Grail, the solution to every problem at the bottom line?

I started to doubt that what we did mattered as much as I used to think it did.

Like the self-storage company executive I met years later, I was tired of it all. I wanted to be doing something that would last, something that was real. Landing the next big client, generating more sales, winning more awards, landing bigger clients...my hamster wheel just kept spinning, and it wasn't working for me anymore.

There had to be something more than this.

Does that sound familiar?

I've talked to thousands of leaders since then about this looming, hollow sense of dread, and many of them are struggling with these same questions. Leadership feels out of control. Business practices feel out of date. There's a pervasive sense of nervousness still clouding over businesses that just barely survived the recession. Everyone does their jobs with their eyes on the bottom line, and in many cases, it looks like it's working. Companies are making money. But yet the CEOs and executives I talk to can feel cracks in the base of their workdays, and the fissures are growing. It feels like we're missing something.

I hear the same questions over and over: *Is this all there is? Can I keep doing this, chasing a bigger bottom line, every day for the next ten, twenty, or forty years?*

And the personal concerns are reflected in the larger, company-wide question:

If our business disappeared tomorrow, would anyone even notice?

Too often, now, the answer is no.

We're not doing anything that truly matters.

To understand why, we need to start thinking beyond the bottom line and the next transaction, and we need to rediscover our own humanity.

In the advertising business I lovingly call home, we've become absolute masters of fancy-sounding but meaningless jargon. *Heads in beds, hands behind the wheels, butts in seats.* We've taught businesses to slice, dice, group, and cluster folks. White, single, head of household, college educated, city dwellers…when was the last time we stopped to think about that list of qualities as an actual person?

With all our research prowess and high-speed connectivity, we don't have a clue about the hearts of our customers. Some companies seem to have forgotten their customers even have a heart, and not just a wallet.

ANOTHER WAY TO LEAD

Joe's business was growing, but without the human component they weren't going anywhere. His employees were miserable and his customers were dissatisfied because they didn't have a clear set of values to guide them.

That conversation in the CEO's office has led to a year-long exploration and articulation of the company's values—something bigger than a dollar sign or an individual whim. It involved everyone in the company. They needed a purpose to dig out of their defensive holes and reconnect with what really mattered.

It's too early to call their turnaround a success, but progress is steady. For the team members who chose to commit to change, change is happening. Joe has a new energy in his voice, and he doesn't talk to me about dying anymore. Instead, we talk about the next twenty years.

Joe discovered that there is another way to lead—one that's about more than another fancy ad campaign or shareholder report.

Are you ready to take a risk and explore a more rewarding way to do business? If you're willing to upend the entire way you do business, shifting to the Values Economy can help you build both meaning into your work life and dollars to your bottom line. It can give you new levels of energy, enthusiasm, and even hope.

But the result is a workplace that can survive in the new millennium, and a personal sense of fulfillment that will give you a renewed sense of purpose in your everyday work life.

ONE

THE FAILURE OF THE TRANSACTIONAL ECONOMY

Throughout the twentieth century, American businesses grew at record-setting rates. Profits soared, first with the post-World War II economy and the Baby Boom, and then with the Internet and the dot-com economy. For many, those experiences set the expectation that wealth and business could continue to grow forever. For a long time, it seemed like there was nowhere to go but up.

Get bigger.

Reach further.

Sell more.

For the generations of business leaders before us, competition was limited. Advertising and marketing were practically unnecessary because most businesses were relational. Communication happened face to face and growth was organic—when more people wanted your products, you made more. When you couldn't do it alone, you brought in others to help. When one location wasn't big enough, you opened another. If you wanted your company to succeed, your primary task was to offer something of better quality than your competition. Sure, there were some outlying cases of runaway success among railroad tycoons and gold miners, but in general, business growth was organic, steady, and based on quality. Success happened over time.

Then technology and innovation made us faster, more efficient, and more globally connected. With the explosion of television and retail chains, our boundaries shifted and very little was entirely local anymore. In response, an emerging field of marketers and advertisers sold *feelings* instead of baking soda and station wagons.

Business stopped being personal as it spread to a wider audience than any CEO could possibly imagine. Customers' loyalties shifted. Community members became global consumers, with access to a variety of products that were, generally speaking, equally adequate. (Did it really matter whether you flew on Pan Am or American Airlines in 1962? Both were filled with young, pretty stewardesses and a cloud of cigarette smoke.)

With the advent of mass communication, interstate transportation, and the consumer bubble of mid-century prosperity, America settled firmly into a transactional economy. I had something you want to buy, and you had money for what I was selling. Once that interaction—that transaction—was over, we both moved on. Success was judged by the exchange of money for products or services: getting more dollars, more customers, and a richer bottom line.

Most of us in senior leadership roles today learned our trade with a focus on the bottom line, rather than the customer. *The win, the kill, the conquest*— these were the driving motivators of the earliest advertising firms I worked for, led by executives who could have walked straight off the set of *Mad Men*. They were the originators of the American obsession with brands and marketing. They taught my generation, one TV commercial at a time, to treat customers like consumers. We thought more about the sale and the product, and less about the person on the other side of the transaction.

In advertising, our job was to build awareness, consideration, trial and, ultimately, that *purchase*. Our emphasis was on acquisition. Our clients hired us to create something shiny and distracting to get people in the door. Our mission was to make the sale and nothing more. What happened after the transaction wasn't our problem.

We were like the person who invests all of their time and money in wooing their special someone, planning for each moment spent together and building the intensity of the relationship all the way to the altar—without putting any time or reflection into the marriage that follows.

THE FIVE Ps

We were selling more and more, and watching the profits benefit fewer and fewer people. In the age of Wall Street, as the fictional Gordon Gecko said in the movie of the same name, "Greed, for lack of a better word, is good."

Technology improved efficiency, accelerated growth, and connected cultures in unprecedented ways. It also introduced new ways to chase transactions, without limits to time or scope. Isolated behind screens and usernames, growing too big to know their employees, let alone their customers, leaders lost sight of their humanity and purpose. Corporations "too big to fail" started to get reckless in their pursuit of success.

Business in the transactional economy was grounded in what has been called the Five P's:

Power

Position

Prestige

Pleasure

Prosperity

The transactional economy flourished for a time, and the Five Ps became ingrained in our culture. They became the ideal. Today, advertisers tantalize us with the possibility of their attainment. The media glamorizes the results of having them.

In and of themselves, there's nothing wrong with these words. Human nature is to seek pleasure. Capitalism drives us toward prosperity. But at their core, the five P's have two major problems.

First, each of these ideas in the wrong hands is **self-focused**. Transactional success is measured by how it benefits either a specific person (*my* power, *my* prestige) or a single company (*our* position, *our* stock price prosperity) in the immediate sense. The focus is on instant gratification, and it doesn't take into account the wider consequences. The perceived winners in the transactional economy don't consider whether winning happens at the expense of someone else, even their own customers. Here, the ends really do justify the means.

Second, the Five Ps are all defined as **outcomes**. Power and position and the rest are *results*, things to try to attain, but there aren't obvious or automatic ways to know when you've arrived. We're always running on the hamster wheel, trying to get to the promised reward, but there's no clear welcome sign to tell us we've arrived. Someone will always have more power, more pleasure, and definitely more prosperity.

15

Self-focused outcomes fail to ask broader, system-wide questions. What guides you as you make difficult, pressure-filled choices every day if your only measuring stick is how much you got for yourself today, or this quarter? Where does our quest for pleasure or prosperity affect our relationships with others? How far should an individual person or corporation go in order to achieve power or prestige?

In the transaction economy, there's no thought to the long term. Stock holders, board members, and even customers judge success on immediate results, record-breaking products, and a rapidly expanding bottom line. As the stakes and expectations get higher, CEOs and leaders race to keep up. More and more, they operate on fear and faking it.

Make the sale. Increase the profit. Expand to new markets. Raise the value before the next quarterly report or shareholder meeting. Build fast. Sell high. Relationships take too much time. Don't bother with infrastructure; you won't be around long enough to need it. Just sell more units. When these are the only things that drive you or your company, they'll relentlessly drive you toward a fall.

No wonder so many of us are left asking if this is all worth it.

Left with the Five Ps and our own uncertainty, without a wider perspective or a moral compass, the race for the transaction can become an exercise in self interest, greed, and expediency, and the validator of horrific behavior.

Fortunately, times have changed, and so have attitudes. The Five Ps are no longer the only way to define success. Many marketers, me included, now see the transaction as the *beginning* of a relationship, not the end. We recognize that the hardest question for people in business today isn't "how do I get it?" It's "how do I keep it?"

I was reminded of that recently when I had lunch with an acquaintance.

16

He was lamenting that his company, a service provider, was experiencing a 60% customer churn rate. They were spinning their wheels faster and faster, trying to bring in enough new customers to keep the doors open, but subscribers were abandoning them faster than they could be replaced.

Knowing that kind of loss wasn't sustainable, I asked if he would let The Values Institute look at what was happening. He agreed, and we launched an internal review of their processes. What we discovered was a business grounded in the old-fashioned, transactional mindset that was all about the initial sale. The company invested huge amounts of money in special discounts, sales, flashy campaigns, and high-pressure promotions for first-time subscribers. The staff tracked new subscribers in real time, posted numbers on the walls, and celebrated success. Sales teams got bonuses. It was an expensive program, to the point where they often lost money.

Once a customer made the purchase, they were shifted to a different department, in another office. The tempting new sales price expired after a few months, and subscription rates rose sharply. Unlike the sales team, the customer service workers who staffed the phone banks operated with a strict script of options. Long-term, loyal customers simply couldn't get the rewards and recognition that new clients did. While the sales team prioritized answering phone calls from potential subscribers on the first telephone ring, the understaffed service team for existing customers constantly had a queue of customers stuck on hold. Systems were difficult to navigate and inflexible. While the sales team was monetarily rewarded for each new customer, customer service representatives were paid minimum wage, with no incentives. Their phone calls were timed, and their metrics tracked, down to the second, to see how quickly they handled the "problems."

The longer a customer stayed with the company, the less the company offered them. Customers were seen as transactions, not people, and they reacted by walking away. What was hidden behind the antiseptic "business-ese" word *churn* was a much more human failing of hurting other human beings.

I went back to my acquaintance and told him, "Your problem here isn't churn. It's a violation of trust."

THE FINAL STRAW

It's probably not a coincidence that my interest in looking at business through the lens of relationships and values started after 9-11 and culminated in the mid-2000s. Trust—or the lack of it—was all over the news. Institutions were imploding. Corporate greed was wreaking havoc.

Enron, the seventh-largest company in the United States, collapsed in a scandal of conspiracy and accounting fraud. The housing crisis that emerged from the subprime mortgages and predatory lending practices, exemplified by the investment bank Lehman Brothers' bankruptcy, threw the entire country into a recession. Those were the dark years when even the queen of homemaking, Martha Stewart, failed us, going to jail for insider trading.

But it was Bernie Madoff's Ponzi scheme, revealed in December 2008, which pushed many of us over the edge and made us take a hard look at what was happening. The former NASDAQ chairman perpetuated the largest financial fraud in U.S. history, bilking 4,800 clients—including members of his own family—out of $65 billion dollars. It was a shocking case of personal betrayal. Madoff didn't just make bad decisions or put a positive spin on a balance sheet. He met people, face to face, and convinced them to hand over their life savings, knowing without a shadow of a doubt that he wasn't going to be able to deliver what he promised them. He lied about how he would deliver above-average profits on retirement accounts and college savings plans, and then he stole their money in order to pay off earlier investors—and this continued for years, possibly decades.

After already enduring so many betrayals, Madoff was the final straw. America had enough with the transactional economy that separated Main Street from Wall Street. The cost of their disillusion came in layers upon layers of new government regulation, with restrictive legislation like Dodd-Frank, costing taxpayers billions of dollars. But more than that, the rampant corruption and abuse of the transaction economy had cost the personal faith of average Americans in the businesses and systems that surrounded us.

By 2015, when the Environmental Protection Agency filed charges against Volkswagen and uncovered their long conspiracy to cheat on emissions tests by intentionally installing "defeat devices" in their diesel passenger cars, allowing cars to release forty times more nitrous oxide than is legally allowed, the public barely seemed surprised. Although Volkswagen's actions were estimated to add enough pollution to cause sixty premature American deaths, and even more in Europe,[1] the streets did not fill with protestors. A few people were fired. The stock price plunged by one-third. But the attention carried a cynical, suspicious attitude that I didn't remember feeling a decade before. Just a few weeks after the scandal broke, the media headlines had moved on to predicting Volkswagen's comeback and asking "Do Other Automakers Cheat?" The attitude seemed to be "well, of course they put their own profits over human lives. Isn't that what business does?"

We've elevated the transaction so far that we've lost our humanity in the process.

A few years ago, I saw a news photo of a young protestor in the Occupy Wall Street movement. His sign read "Corporate Greed Is a Symptom." That, to me, said it all. Corporate America had created and celebrated a system that rewarded profit at any cost, and that had left millions of hard-working professionals behind. And now those Americans are abandoning the system.

Far beyond mere financial bankruptcy, the decades of corporate scandals leave us reeling from a values bankruptcy that is like a tsunami, washing us out to sea carried by a strong cultural current of self interest.

We were drowning. We'd lost jobs. We'd lost billions of dollars. But most of all, we'd lost trust.

REJECTING THE TRANSACTIONAL ECONOMY

The transactional economy failed us. Its leaders, and there are plenty who remain, are out of touch, driven by obscure goals that can never be met, and racing after immediate gratification that melts like cotton candy.

America, in turn, is rejecting the transactional economy.

From the moment we wake up, the average American is bombarded with logos, advertising, and products all designed to gain our business and our loyalty, yet research shows that as a community we view most brands as insignificant. If businesses and brands are going to seek only their own advancement, without doing anything to make their customers' lives better, then people aren't going to do anything to support the brand.

The majority of people worldwide wouldn't care if 73% of all brands disappeared tomorrow. In the U.S. that number is even worse: they would gladly give up 92% of brands completely.[2]

Stop. Read those numbers again. This should be a crushing statement to every person who works in a consumer-facing business. It speaks to the very heart of why you're here, reading this book. If it doesn't make you pause to think that your company's very existence does not mean anything to the majority of people today, I don't know what will.

Not convinced? What if you replaced "brand" with "people?" Because that's what a brand is—it's the name and image that represent the hopes and futures of real people. If we take away that de-humanizing language that tries to keep business focused on the transaction, what I see here is that most people wouldn't care if *I* disappeared tomorrow.

That's not the way I want to live.

And the seismic shift of expectations isn't just affecting customers. Employees, too, are feeling the lack of commitment. The media is full of reports about the shocking income gap between rich and poor; the average CEO of a Fortune 500 company makes 350 times as much as the average worker.[3] But equally concerning is the growing *trust* gap between senior-level executives and the rank and file in organizations:

Only 43% of employees think that their CEO is a credible source of information about their company.[4]

Almost half of all employees do not trust their senior managers or CEOs, and two-thirds believe senior managers do not care how their employees perceive them.[5]

Sixty percent of Americans believe that corporate corruption remains widespread in boardrooms across America.[6]

And the Human Resource department, which should be the bastion of employee advocacy, is distrusted by more than half of all executives and senior managers, and almost 70% of all hourly employees.[7]

The income divide is a symbol of a larger psychological chasm, where employees struggle with a lack of communication, a lack of vision, and often a lack of respect. Workers today often feel like cannon fodder, and so they disengage.

In 2006, the year that The Values Institute began our research, a *Gallup Management Journal* survey revealed that only 29% of employees considered themselves actively engaged in their jobs, working with passion and feeling a profound connection to their company. The rest, a painful 71%, were either "not engaged" or "actively disengaged." At best, they were plodding through their workdays and putting time—but not passion—into their work. At worst, they were actively acting out their unhappiness, undermining whatever their more engaged, passionate coworkers were accomplishing.[8]

It throws a dark light onto the old joke: A CEO was asked how many people work in his company: "About half of them," he responded.

And there's a final death blow to the transaction economy: most people are just not interested in transactions themselves anymore. After decades of amassing as much stuff as possible, conspicuous consumption is dead. Half of all adult respondents in a global survey said they'd happily live without most of the items they own.[9] We're buying less, purchasing fewer packaged goods, downsizing out of our McMansions, and generally staying out of shopping malls.[10] Perhaps it's because income hasn't kept pace with the cost increases of necessities like health care and housing, or we're concerned about the environmental impact of over-consumption. But I believe that it's also because we're overwhelmed by the personal impact of so much *stuff.*

Journalist Joel Stein says that it's because "material goods have gotten so cheap, they've become burdensome,"[11] reminding me of a century-old quote from Bertrand Russell: "It is preoccupation with possessions, more than anything else, that prevents us from living freely and nobly."

And that was back before the crisis of the salad dressing aisle.

No longer do we live in a world of vinegar and oil, three television networks, and tap water. There are now over one hundred salad dressings in my local supermarket and a dozen different brands of bottled water (not including the ones that come with flavors). Hundreds of cable TV channels give me so many choices that my head spins faster than my former friend, the turntable.

When offered so many choices, they all start to look alike. This is what we call the *sea of sameness*. Categories offer little, if anything, to differentiate most products. Is there really a difference among those dozen brands of Italian salad dressing? Will this brand of printer paper really be noticeably different than the one over there?

When we're drowning in options that all look the same, we're likely to take a dimmer view of all of them.

Psychologist and author Barry Schwartz has studied this explosion of choice, and in his book *The Paradox of Choice*, he concludes that there is a point where too many options makes us not freer and happier, but paralyzed and dissatisfied. We know that it's almost impossible to make the "right" choice anymore, and so we just don't make any choice at all. Mr. Schwartz attributes much of the depression found at rampant levels in America today to our inability to choose wisely. And when we do choose, full of expectations created by the impression that so many options means that there must be one perfect choice, we're invariably let down by reality.

It's just another way that the transactions with our brands disappoint us.

These consumer revolts against the transaction economy are being led by the youngest adults, the Millennial Generation, so the changes are likely here to stay. Today's twenty- and thirty-somethings grew up in a society that was already hyper-saturated with brand advertising and messaging, and they quickly learned to tune it out. Their first exposure to business came from those stories of Wall Street scandal and betrayal, and they categorically rejected the idea of working for a business that exists for no purpose other than making money. Millennials are more likely to be influenced by peer reviews, not splashy banners or "expert" opinions. They trust the people they know, and the groups that share their values—not the messages brands bombard them with at every opportunity. They recognize the same bag of tricks, the same superficial goods and services, and they're not having it.

THE BEGINNING OF MY JOURNEY

There I was, in the late 2000s, in my increasingly uncomfortable seat in advertising, observing all of this. I was starting to realize that I was part of the problem, selling goods and services as if they were critical to people's happiness. My entire career was built around the transaction, but what I was longing for, and what I heard others longing for, wasn't another product. We wanted to trust the people around us again. We wanted to know how to make a lasting difference in the businesses we worked with, and by extension with our clients and customers. We wanted to have conversations about things that mattered, and that were bigger than the features on the latest gadget.

Again, we had great clients who were giving us creative, interesting work. But advertising more stuff—even good stuff—wasn't an effective way to fight back against the trust violations all around me. I wanted something else, something that could fundamentally change the things that I saw that were wrong in business. I wanted to transcend the immediate gratification of selling more products and services, and uncover the key to sustainable satisfaction.

Late one afternoon, after everyone else had gone home, I confided my thoughts in a colleague, my good friend Chesley Beaver. It was a conversation that changed my life.

Chesley served as the agency's Director of Strategic Planning, but he was also a bit of a Renaissance man, with, among other things, a master's degree in sociology. When I mentioned that I was interested in doing some research into how to transcend all of the trust violations and dysfunctional corporate scandals, he lit up. Chesley loved research.

I asked him, "How can some companies act without a conscience? And what can we do to change that?" I wanted to find a way to stand for something bigger than the next transaction, and to reposition ourselves and the clients we served. But after a lifetime of working within the old system, I had no idea where to start.

Chesley thought about it for a minute. "You know, if we really want to find answers, we can't come at it like marketers. We can't have that hat on, because we know that marketing and sales are part of the problem. What we're really talking about here is a way to better understand human behavior and relationships."

That was the first time that I'd truly connected with the word *relationship* in conjunction with marketing, as something that transcended the transaction. Today, there are other people talking about the importance of building relationships between customers and brands. But back then, Chesley was on to something radical and untested.

Intuitively, we agreed that what was missing from our experience as business leaders, and as consumers, was the sense of accountability and purpose that comes with being human. Every CEO, we agreed, is a human being who desires successful relationships. Every customer is a person who desires to be understood. Most of us, in my experience, want to live with integrity, and appreciate others who feel the same.

Yet our interactions as buyers and sellers, or employers and employees, no longer felt connected to our humanity. We weren't respected, and we weren't respecting others. We weren't working for a reason. And that was leaving us feeling like we were drowning.

He kept talking. "The formula is simple: if you have a healthy relationship, you'll have multiple transactions. If your relationship is diseased, or you don't have any relationship at all, you might get one or two sales if you're lucky. But it can't sustain itself."

I was hooked.

TWO

LEARNING THE LANGUAGE
OF RELATIONSHIPS

A re you familiar with the scene in most epic action movies, where the crusading hero gathers like-minded men of valor to fight for the just cause? Well, that's how I feel about that late-afternoon conversation with Chesley. I didn't know it at the time, but Chesley had already decided that he wanted to move away from his career in advertising, and he was looking for new, more socially meaningful projects. I'd just placed one in his lap.

Chesley helped me discover the academic understanding that our sense of humanity comes, in part, from relationships. Humans come into the world as relational beings, and we instinctively seek social and emotional connections that are rewarding in both tangible and intangible ways. It's such a core part of who we are that to not have it is devastating. We measure our personal health, at least in part, on the depth and sustainability of those relationships. The old expression "no man is an island" is absolutely true—without relationships we atrophy and die.

27

The research backed it up. One meaningful study followed more than 309,000 people, and found that a lack of strong relationships increased their risk of premature death by a full 50%—that's roughly comparable to smoking fifteen cigarettes a day, and is more fatal than both obesity and physical inactivity.[12] Other studies show that social relationships introduce accountability and encourage positive behavior, adding even more value.[13]

If no person is an island, and we agreed that businesses and brands were, at the core, collections of people, then it served to reason that no brand could successfully exist as an island, either. When we're isolated, either personally or corporately, we atrophy.

Chesley and I hypothesized that the strains we saw in the business world and the cracks we felt in our own careers came from a lack of priority on relationships—let alone other human beings—in the workplace, where Americans spent so much of our time and intellectual effort. After all, we're the same people at work that we are at home. A lot of the relationships that we experience every day, whether it's with a colleague or a coffee shop barista, are related somehow to business and work. The way we're treated affects us. The way we think about them affects our sense of harmony and balance.

Yet what we consider critical in our homes and social lives—warmth, respect, and understanding—seem to be disappearing on the morning commute, and what we are left with is impersonal, transactional, and sometimes even abusive. Our conclusion was that we can't spend one-third to one-half of every week acting in ways that contradict a base need. Our emotional wiring doesn't change when we're sitting at a conference room table. It doesn't disappear when we grab a basket at the grocery store.

Even a healthy network of family and friends—which Chesley and I both had—couldn't make up for so much time spent ignoring the humanity around us.

We were paying too much attention to the transactions, and not enough to the people behind them. Bringing relationships and humanity back into the workplace could have immediate, tangible benefits on our current, struggling state of corporate misbehavior and mistrust.

But what did that mean? It was more than just being nicer to coworkers and customers. That was good advice, but it didn't address the lack of purpose we felt in the hamster wheel. How could this idea of relationships fundamentally change not just the way we act, but the way we do business?

Over the next year, the partners and senior members of our agency spent every spare minute exploring this idea of relationships: what they were, how they worked, and what that had to do with the miserable state of the world today. What began innocently as my desire to re-purpose my own career track and reposition our advertising agency ended up changing the way that we looked at our company, our personal relationships, and even each other. It made us redefine success. It spun us both into new, more meaningful projects.

And it led me to a revelation called the Values Economy.

RELATIONSHIPS AND THE WORKPLACE

If we could figure out how to connect our humanity back to our transactions, perhaps we could find a way to bring integrity and sustainability back to the workplace.

From the start of our research, we agreed to the somewhat novel idea that relationships are not exclusively interpersonal, and that **a business or a brand is also capable of—and dependent on—relationships,** and that **corporate relationships are likely to grow or fail for the same reasons that personal relationships do**. After all, a corporation is, by legal definition, a *collection of people* who come together to accomplish a common project or goal. The umbrella title of "corporation" exists not to shield us from our desire for relationships, but to help people work collectively while avoiding personal risk and limiting liability. That truth has been lost in the fast-paced, cutthroat world of the transactional economy.

Individuals—from the senior leaders to the entry-level employees—bring to their work our collective, human, healthy desire for connection and meaning. We all need relationships in our business life. Our humanity draws us to relate with our customers, employees, and even other businesses. When that desire for relationships is ignored or misused, the resulting disconnect creates a vacuum where mistakes are made.

We only need to look at the news to know that too many leaders hide behind fancy logos, shielding themselves from the moral and emotional repercussions of acting in unconscionable ways. This is, in part, what brought us to the corporate crises and scandals of the early twenty-first century. But by the time Chesley and I started our project, the tide was turning. Individuals were once again being held accountable for what they did. After all, Enron and Worldcom might have failed, but it was Jeffrey Skilling and Bernie Ebbers who went to jail.

If businesses that ignored their need for relationship failed, it followed that a business that prioritized healthy relationships would benefit, just as individuals do. A business that enjoyed strong connections with both customers and employees would be able to build loyalty, which would sustain it during difficult times. It could offer leaders accountability and positive social pressures as they make daily decisions that could help—or harm— others. And, most importantly of all, relationships would provide a group of people who are working and interacting together with a sense of purpose and direction that went beyond the transaction.

Intuitively, we could point to companies that seemed to understand the value of relationships. While major brands were collapsing like dominoes, workers were being laid off by the thousands, CEOs were being carted off in handcuffs, and the rest of us were left wondering if there was anything to believe in anymore, some companies were charging forward. Their businesses were growing, and their customers and employees seemed happy. Starbucks, a brand built on providing places of "warmth and belonging," seemed to get it. Apple's sleek, friendly Genius Bars broke down barriers and treated employees and customers with respect. And it wasn't just national brands. We could look at local service organizations, from healthcare providers to lawn care companies, and say "yep, they're relational," or "no, I don't get that sense of connection from them." We could meet a CEO and sense, within five minutes, whether he cared about connections or was just looking at a bottom-line number. In those difficult days, the companies that cared shone like beacons.

What we didn't know was *why*. What made these companies special? Did they throw a lot of money into human resources? Did they buy different kinds of ads? Did their leaders all go on special retreats? How did an organization become a business built on humanity instead of a business built on transaction?

The first step was to establish a general understanding of how relationships work.

We started by asking each other questions about our own meaningful relationships in order to develop a baseline of observations—what attracted you to your wife? Why is your best friend your best friend? Who has betrayed a relationship, and how did that end?

Then we extended our research. As social scientists, we wanted to collect qualitative data to help us find patterns and recognize common elements. As advertising guys, our natural way to research was through interviews and focus groups. So we invited our own employees, from account managers to administrative staff, to talk to us about their relationships. We heard some wonderful stories, as well as a few heartbreaking ones.

We asked each person to describe their very best personal relationship, and then to tell us about a relationship that was completely disastrous. We heard about lovers, parents, spouses, siblings, and friends. Over and over, we heard similar themes about the kinds of valuable connections that brought people together at a deeper-than-surface level.

The first thing we noticed was the difference between infatuation and real relationships. Despite the fairy tale stories, none of our subjects chose to talk about "love at first sight." What mattered to them was much more complicated. Sure, maybe a first date went well because of physical chemistry or a shared hobby. Perhaps a person was "swept off their feet" by an incredibly generous gift or offer. But physical attraction fades quickly, and hobbies change. For an initial experience to deepen into one of the most important relationships in a person's life, we saw, they had to reach something more personal. Developing a meaningful connection wasn't really about whether two people both enjoyed sushi. Healthy, beautiful relationships were based on how two people expressed themselves together, and how each person responded.

The relationships that stuck were deeply connected to how a person perceived themselves, as well as the other person. Over and over, we heard words like *honesty*, *vulnerability*, and *advocacy*.

"She thinks like I do."

"He understood what I was trying to say."

"We cared about the same things."

"I could be myself."

"I **trusted** her."

HOW TRUST DEVELOPS

We noticed that one word—trust—came up over and over. We also heard about a lot of relationships that failed because of a lack of trust. *He was jealous. She walked out. He took. She betrayed me.*

It captivated us, and spoke to the questions we were asking. But what did it tell us about our work lives?

Today, marketers throw *trust* around like it's any other buzzword. Ford Motor Company touted "trust is the new black" as one of their "13 trends to watch in 2013:"

If trust were bottled as wine, the vintages of recent years would be bitter—and scarce... More important than ever to building brand equity and differentiation, trust has become a precious commodity, and its limited supply in the marketplace has stimulated consumer demand.[14]

But ten years ago, Chesley and I felt like two advertising guys trying to learn a whole new language. We knew, based on dozens of similar definitions, that trust was a *belief in the reliability, ability, or strength of someone or something.* We noted that there was a certain amount of risk involved in trust; it reveals itself only when we offer something of ourselves. We expect that the other party will act in a certain way, but we can't guarantee it. Trust isn't about regulations or force. It's about not needing those things.

Trust, we concluded, is what differentiates a healthy, long-term relationship from something fleeting and shallow that never develops. Those companies that were shining in the darkness had earned the trust of their employees and customers.

When we looked at it with our business hats on, a few other things also stood out to us about what trust *wasn't*.

Trust doesn't lie. "Honesty is a very expensive gift," says Warren Buffett. "Don't expect it from cheap people." Trust develops when we discover, through trial and error, where we can be ourselves, and where we can be vulnerable. Trust happens when we reveal something that's deeper than the surface. In a trusting relationship we are the honest person who lives behind the polite image that we share with strangers. We feel like someone understands us and won't judge us. We admit when we screw up.

This is a hard message for businesses to embrace. We trained generations of leaders to package and present a "public face" of their business, and to control and spin every scrap of information, every income report, and every press release. Instead of building trust in a relationship, we told them to dominate. Vulnerability, to them, sounds like letting competitors see the weakness, or the vulnerable "underbelly," of an organization. Yet recent studies have proven the benefits of vulnerability between brands and customers. Customer loyalty grows when ordinary people are invited to join user groups, share information, and even help to design public offerings. The reality is that the real danger comes if we maintain distance and hold back our emotions. In those cases, there's no room for trust to grow. Those relationships don't last.

Trust can't be bought. After a divorce, many absent parents try to buy their way out of guilt and into their child's life with expensive gifts. But what children really need from their parents is time, attention, and consistency. When we asked our focus groups how the most meaningful people won their trust, they never talked about boxes wrapped in shiny paper or fancy vacations. Those might earn someone's companionship or presence, but trust went much deeper.

Business relationships work the same way. For years, hotels have been getting guests through the door by offering them special perks and discounts based on a "points" system. But when we surveyed regular hotel customers, it became clear that the points, like every other now-ubiquitous "loyalty membership" program, didn't build customer trust. When they're bribed with points and courted with dollars, hotel guests don't build loyalty to the customer service or the trappings of a particular brand; they build loyalty to the system of points. They believe rooms are interchangeable, and they're ready to jump ship for anyone who gives them a better offer.

A company that has been inconsistent or offensive with its behavior can't rebuild trust by announcing a giant sale. The occasional staff party or free coffee in the break room does not build a relationship between an employer and an employee. Trust takes time, consistency, and transparency.

The deepest levels of trust are not automatically granted. Trust, like friendship or relationship, was a word that came with subtle shades of meaning. We don't offer the same kinds of trust to everyone. So Chesley and I went back to the established research, and discovered that sociologists have outlined different, distinct levels of trust. Most relationships are built on a progression:

At the basest level, **_deterrence-based trust_** unites two people or groups under the promise—or threat—of consistent behavior and threat of punishment. "Deterrence based trust will work only to the degree that punishment is possible, consequences are clear, and the punishment is actually imposed if the trust is violated."[15] This barely fit our definition of trust at all, but it is the level at which many brands and leaders operate. Deterrence is the motivator used to bring two antagonistic or self-focused parties together to accomplish a goal. It is the reason why we have written contracts that ensure each party can be assured that the other will hold up their end of the bargain, or internal policies and procedures to provide boundaries for how we act with each other. If we break contracts or violate rules, there are consequences.

When American businesses failed to keep their commitments and betrayed the faith of investors and customers, the government stepped in with a deterrence-based set of regulations to keep the system running. Deterrence became the standard among betrayed, suspicious strangers in the transactional economy.

When people get past the lawyers and threats, the first level of personal trust typically exchanged in a new relationship is called **_calculus-based trust_**. We start to offer pieces of ourselves, but we're cautious and unfamiliar. We _calculate_ the possible repercussions of engagement: what are the costs and benefits of sustaining this relationship? What are the costs and benefits of severing it? At first, we keep a governor on our vulnerability and how much we expect from one another, and a single violation or inconsistency can destroy trust and end a relationship before it begins.

Your first visit to a new doctor relies on calculus-based trust. Yes, you've probably checked out the outside indicators of reliability: the doctor has a medical degree, your insurance company considers her safe, you've read all of the online patient reviews, and there's a full waiting room of other patients who seem as content as people in a waiting room can be. But until you know how well the doctor will listen and respond to you, and whether she can recognize your symptoms and follow through in ways that keep you safe and healthy, the trust you're offering is secondhand and therefore unreliable. If the doctor disappoints you, it's easy to walk away and find someone else.

Calculus-based trust only goes as deep as the interaction of the moment, and it can vanish as quickly as it appears. That's something that popular NBC News anchor Brian Williams learned, when investigations revealed that he'd embellished several stories to make his experience covering the Iraq War appear more dramatic than it was. The public objected. In just a week, Williams dropped from the 23rd most trusted person in America to Number 835.[16] It didn't help that a few months before, to celebrate his ten-year anniversary, TV commercials showed warm images of the newsman talking to soldiers and children while wearing a bulletproof vest. "It's a thing that you build slowly over time," actor Michael Douglas voices over the scenes. "It can happen over big moments, but more often it's the day-to-day things. And what you build if you work hard enough, if you respect it, is a powerful thing called *trust*." [17] His employer had almost no choice but to suspend him for six months and demote him from the coveted nightly news anchor desk.

As time passes and experiences build up, most relationships progress from calculus-based trust to ***knowledge-based trust***, when we know enough about a person, group, or brand to be able to predict their behavior, and believe that they will continue to act consistently and responsibly with

37

what we give them.

Knowledge-based trust is built on our experiences together. This is the level of trust that customers give to their everyday brands, and it's what holds together most coworkers and professional relationships together, with a shared, general understanding of roles and responsibilities. We trust that the products we buy will be safe and consistent, because we've bought a lot of grocery store produce without ever being poisoned. We stop worrying that we need to document every detail or get approval for every decision. At work, after we've seen that our boss respects us and our coworkers can handle their jobs, we let go of some tension or a sense of potential threat; this allows us to focus together on other, bigger issues.

On the end of the spectrum, *identification-based trust* happens when all of those initial questions of stability and consistency have been answered and proven so often, and both parties know each other so well, that we can act on each other's behalf. We can anticipate how the other person will react, because we know how they think and what's important to them. It's like the couple who have been married for so many decades that they can finish each other's sentences.

Identity-based trust can't be the ultimate outcome for every relationship; it's typically reserved for our closest connections. This was what we heard from our focus groups as they described spouses, children, family, and close friends. In certain circumstances, this level of trust can also cross over to the professional or even consumer experiences, and lead to better performance. This mutual understanding reveals a level of trust that goes without even needing to discuss behavior and options. A professional sports team, for instance, demonstrates identification-based trust. Players spend hundreds of hours practicing together, learning how to anticipate each other's motion and movement. They build a common set of experiences that guide their behavior. Identification-based trust is why a football quarterback doesn't throw the ball to where his receiver is standing, but instead launches the ball ahead, to the place where he knows the receiver will be by the time the ball gets there.

The two highest levels of trust, knowledge and identity, are generally achieved through consistency over many shared experiences, as we see in marriages that have survived decades. But sometimes, there were cases where one relationship of trust could support another, and help it jump almost immediately to identification-based trust.

This was made personally clear to me about a year ago, when a friend told me that he really wanted to introduce me to his friend Ron.

"Why?" I asked.

"Because he's so much like you. He loves the same things that you do. And he's a really good friend of mine, and you and I have a great relationship, so I think that you'll like him, too." The endorsement of my friend—who already had my trust—predisposed me to meet Ron. And I'm glad I did, because the very first time we got together, we hit it off. We had an immediate connection, and an almost immediate identification level of trust. We talked for almost three hours, and none of it was casual small talk.

As our relationship has progressed, I've had a chance to reaffirm that first impression, and Ron has never let me down. As I've learned more about who he is and what he believes, I find myself responding to that. As I see how he lives, I find myself more inclined to be real with him.

A year after we met, my wife and I had dinner with Ron and his wife. It was just the four of us, and we'd had a great time, with real conversations that reflected a deep, genuine friendship. I'm not generally one to wear my heart on my sleeve, but as the evening wore on I looked around the table and said, "You know what's so invigorating about spending time with you both is that I feel like I'm really human. There are no guard rails around this friendship, and I feel completely safe."

It was a vulnerable thing for me to say, but I didn't feel vulnerable with them. I wanted them to know why I covet time with them, since most of our time is filled with superficial stuff, and this wasn't. It was real.

I'm not telling you this story because I want to brag about how great my friends are—although they are great. I'm telling you because companies have the same opportunity to connect with customers by being vulnerable, and by being willing to share what really matters to them.

Do your customers know what you stand for? Can your employees point to how the company's values affect their everyday responsibilities? One of the messages we try to convey to all of our agency clients is that you can jump-start your relationship with employees and customers by communicating your values clearly and quickly. If your values statement is hidden on a sub-page of a website, and isn't influencing the message on the home page, then you're missing the opportunity to set expectations.

WHERE DOES CORPORATE TRUST COME FROM?

What makes employees at Costco[18] and Google[19] so happy, while employees of the bookstore chain Books-A-Million and the cable and Internet service provider company Frontier Communications rate their employers as the "worst"[20] to work for? Why do customers consistently rate brands like Johnson & Johnson as trustworthy,[21] and Comcast cable service as "most hated?"[22]

As we studied customer responses to the multitude of surveys about "best" and "worst" companies, we noticed that most customers, when asked to elaborate their strong positive and negative reactions to brands, never brought up transaction-based metrics like cost. They don't decide whether they like a company based on a new subscriber discount. Instead, they're interested in talking about how the company felt to them, or even about them.

"They know what I need and provide it."

"They care about my well being."

"They make every interaction enjoyable."

"They care for me more than they care about me opening my wallet."

"They understand me."

If a customer had a negative incident or experience with a brand—something that could threaten trust—it was the *reaction of the company* to the perceived violation that determined the ultimate perception. And more than that, it was the initial impression that a person had about the company's reaction. If a brand stumbled in action, but maintained the relationship—honoring trust and showing that they cared about the customer—they could be forgiven.

After all, Apple's Genius Bars are tech support for Apple products that aren't working. Yet Apple makes what could be a negative experience—the inconvenience of having to make a special trip to fix a problem—into something that makes the customer feel recognized and important. And they do it every time.

On the other hand, if a brand responds to a trust violation by trying to cover up their mistakes or seeming to want to mislead their customers, the trust bond is broken, and the relationship is often irreparably damaged. Most politicians who sleep around aren't forced out of office because of their sexual misconduct; they're booted when they try to lie and cover up their sins.

Our research was backed up by a larger survey of 8,000 worldwide consumers in 2010.[23] The differences in customer behavior as related to trust are stark: 91% report that they buy products and services from a company they trust, and 55% say that they will even pay a premium to work with their preferred, trusted brand. On the other hand, three out of four respondents refuse to buy products from companies they distrust, and feel comfortable criticizing the brand to friends. Customers clearly make their purchasing decisions based on trust, and their attitude reaches out to influence others.

We asked our focus groups, which by now had extended past our own staff, about trials and times when it seemed like their primary, most valuable personal relationships were at risk. Had there been a violation of trust? If so—and almost every person could describe a period of strain in their best relationships—what kept the relationship together?

Every answer was some variation of:

"We held onto the things that we both believe."

"We focused on the things that were important to both of us."

Healthy relationships, then, were built on trust. And trust was not just built by time or consistent behavior. It was based on something bigger—**something that encompasses who we are as people, and as groups.**

Generation after generation has had to learn the hard way that the Five Ps are not sufficient. Profits do not bring contentment. Growth does not satisfy. Just ask John D. Rockefeller, America's first billionaire and the richest man of his time. When he was asked, "How much is enough?" he answered, "Just a little bit more." Toward the end of his life, he said, "I have made many millions, but they have brought me no happiness. I would barter them all for the days I sat on an office stool in Cleveland and counted myself rich on three dollars a week."

A hundred years later, the current world's richest man, Bill Gates, concurred. When asked if it would bother him to not be the world's richest man anymore, Gates responded, "I wish I wasn't, there's nothing good that comes out of that."[24]

The solution to the problem of trust wasn't money, and it wasn't time, and it wasn't even something as straightforward as integrity or following the rules. For real, lasting, business-changing, life-changing change, we needed to get down to the core of a person or company's identity, and find the community who connected with it.

We needed to talk about values.

PLANTING OUR FLAG

In our personal lives it's values that define our character, and in our corporate lives those same values define our culture.

The key to sustainability would come from a company's very identity and what mattered most to it. The pieces—the customer's hesitancy and the leader's longing for something more intentional— were in place. We saw the opportunity for a revolution of business practices, and we took it.

I called the staff of the agency together. I started out by talking about one of my favorite movies, *National Treasure*, with Nicholas Cage. I described the scene where he put on special glasses and suddenly he could see all of the invisible writing on the back of the Declaration of Independence. That experience changed everything he thought he knew about American history.

I told my employees, "Today I'm going to give you a set of glasses of your own. You're not advertising professionals anymore. I want you to be social scientists. I want you to see all of our clients through that lens. From here out, we will look for connection points, not products. We'll talk about their identity, not their services. We'll tell their story, and uncover their values."

The staff, thankfully, was excited about the new direction. As we'll explore in later chapters, brands can't grow meaningful relationships outside until they've established a common purpose internally. Together, we tested some ways to approach values-based marketing with a few existing clients who were game to be guinea pigs, and I immediately felt a change in the atmosphere. Instead of talking about the pixel size of the product image in the next ad, we were asking more probing, deeper questions about why the company made this product in the first place. The campaigns were different—and wildly successful.

We had found a new fuel, a different perspective.

It was a risk. The agency had a full roster of clients who liked it when we designed a catchy new slogan or an attention-getting billboard. They'd never talked to us—or often anyone—about their values before. Some of them didn't want to change. When I met with our existing client base, and when we pitched our services to new accounts, there were plenty of marketing managers and CEOs whose eyes would glaze over as soon as we stopped talking about numbers and sales. They weren't interested in "soft" topics like values and customer relationships. We learned that those weren't the clients we worked well with, anyway.

In their place, we discovered there were plenty of businesses who were drawn to what we were saying. Like Joe back in the introduction, they could feel the cracks in their models. They knew that something was broken inside, and they longed for someone to help them, even a small ad agency in Southern California.

"I knew you were right for us within the first five minutes," said one CEO of a multi-billion dollar company. "I'd requested proposals from every agency in the area, and every single presentation felt exactly the same. They were all going to *increase awareness, create trial,* and *drop more to the bottom line.* But your message was different. You put your stake in the ground, but it wasn't about yourself or how fast you could make us money. You talked about my company, our values, and who we were. That's what I'm looking for, and I didn't even know it."

Welcome to the Values Economy.

THREE

THE VALUE OF
SHARED VALUES

Howard Schultz grew up in one of the rougher neighborhoods of Brooklyn. When he was seven years old, his father, Fred, slipped on the ice while he was working as a diaper service driver and broke his leg. Fred's employer fired him immediately, with no severance or benefits. (Back in 1960, there were no workman's comp laws.) Without health insurance and with the elder Schultz unable to work, the family struggled for years to make ends meet. Fred Schultz never fully recovered, mentally or physically.

Howard went on to college on a football scholarship, and became the first member of his family to earn a degree. In 1987, he bought a small Seattle coffee roaster called Starbucks Coffee Company. The company sold roasted beans, but not prepared coffee. Schultz wanted to change that. Inspired by the ritual and sense of community he'd felt in Italy's espresso bars, he set out to bring the idea to America of a community environment that, according to company literature, "not only celebrated coffee and the rich tradition, but that also *brought a feeling of connection*."[25]

That was the business plan. For Schultz, though, his company's real *purpose* wasn't to roast and serve the perfect bean; it was to create a culture that treated all people with dignity and respect. When asked in a 2013 interview with Oprah Winfrey about his vision for the company, he said it's "not the calling of coffee, but the calling to try to build a company that my father never got a chance to work for.... When we began Starbucks, what I wanted to try to do was to create a set of values, guiding principles, and culture."

At Starbucks, people on the payroll are not called employees or workers; from the barista-in-training to the senior VP, they're all *partners*. The company became, according to Schultz, the first in the United States to offer comprehensive health insurance and ownership in the form of stock options to part-time as well as full-time workers. In recent years they've launched programs to pay for college education, to recruit and train military veterans, and to provide forums for discussing difficult topics like race.

Their culture is succeeding. Forty-five years after the first store opened in Seattle, Starbucks has more than 20,000 stores in 66 countries, employing 182,000 people and serving tens of millions of customers. It has weathered recessions, leadership changes, the occasional controversy, and remains one of the most globally-recognized brands in the world.

What's the secret of their success? According to Schultz, it's all about values. "We live in a sea of mediocrity in all walks of life," Schultz said in an interview with the *Harvard Business Review*. "We also live amid a fracturing of civility... Everywhere we go as consumers, we're getting people who don't want to reach into our hearts or know who we are; they want to reach into our wallets and get some money. The equity of the [Starbucks] brand is defined by the quality of the coffee but also, most importantly, by the relationship that the barista has with the customer and whether or not the customer feels valued, appreciated, and respected. That is our aspiration every day."[26]

COMPETENCE AND CONSISTENCY AREN'T ENOUGH

Chesley and I weren't the only ones who were recognizing the need to develop a stronger culture of trust in a troubled economy. After the Madoff scandal pushed Americans past the point of what they would tolerate, the market flooded with books urging brands to exhibit integrity and transparency as a way to win back suspicious customers. More leaders wanted to talk to me about building trust. They accepted, at least in theory, that a tide was turning.

But many of them struggled with how to do it. I've talked to plenty of business owners and executives, in companies of all sizes and purposes, who are still floundering almost a decade into this new culture of openness. *Mike, I don't know what's missing. Our company's reputation is clean; no scandals, no bankruptcies, no bad press. We kept our prices stable through the recession, gave our employees the best benefit package we could afford, and filed all of our financial disclosure paperwork. We're not upsetting anyone. We're consistent. But yet there's no spark here. We're losing customers. Why isn't it working?*

There's nothing wrong with being competent and consistent. In fact, as we continue to work through this discussion of trust and values, you'll see that those two components are the very foundation of trust. And in times of crisis and uncertainty, like in the last recession, this was what customers expected, and were willing to accept.

When things were hard, customers and employees needed to know, at the very least, that a person and a business would do what they said they would do, and would do it well. Without that, nothing else mattered. But as The

Values Institute talked to consumers year after year for our Most Trustworthy Brands Survey, we also saw that as consumers became more stable post-recession, competence and consistency, alone, stopped being enough. They became the ante to get in the game.

The reality is that there are plenty of companies that are consistent and competent. Because of technology, regulation, better communication, or some combination of the three, my daily, first world life is free from most real danger. My environment protects me from most extremes, and keeps me safe from most risks. I can confidently eat the fruit from any of the grocery stores and farmers markets in my county, knowing that there are food safety regulations in place to make sure it won't harm me. I drive by at least five FDIC-insured banks on my commute to work every day; I can deposit my money into any of them and know that it won't disappear in an economic collapse. I can buy a high-quality wool sweater from any of a dozen different specialty clothing companies, and the results will, generally speaking, be equally good. If my company lays me off, I can get another job.

Now, people want more. They want a company they can trust to stand for something. When we're flooded with companies that all competently make a consistently good toaster, that's no longer enough to draw our loyalty. We raise the stakes, consciously or subconsciously, on what we look for. We start to want something bigger than a toaster.

We want a company that **shares our values.**

Sure, Starbucks baristas competently pull a consistently good espresso shot, but that's not why customers are willing to pay four dollars for a cup of coffee day after day. What draws coffee drinkers to gather under the mermaid logo is the *value* that the company has put on community, and the role they've taken in providing a place for it to flourish. Starbucks' commitment to respect their partners, their customers, and their neighbors is what makes the brand ubiquitous. It's what has drawn millions of people to trust them.

In a 2012 *Harvard Business Review* survey, **64% of American consumers cite shared values as the reason why they have a relationship with a brand**.[27] And according to the 2014 Harris Poll Reputation Quotient, more than half the American public seek information about the ethics and behavior of companies that they hear about or do business with, and 36% say that they've decided against doing business with a company because of something they learned.[28]

For a business to establish itself in a sustainable, long-term way in this new Values Economy, it needs to be more than consistent; it needs to successfully live in a relationship with its constituents. And just as we saw in our earliest focus group feedback, the way to build long-term trust within that relationship is to *share something* and *stand for something* that's bigger than the transaction. This shared space of purpose is where the electricity happens, where the joy happens, and where the peace and calm and stability come from.

Creating meaning instead of merely creating a product is the gateway to sustainable growth. Your values form an almost impenetrable shield that can surround your internal and external relationships. Without a sense of purpose, your best employees are vulnerable to better offers. Your competition can replicate your manufacturing process and offer cheaper knockoffs of your product. Your customers can be lured by a better sale, an easier location, or just the shiny distraction of something new. But trust can't be bought or sold. Competitors can't replicate or fight against trust. Customers find it hard to abandon.

Your values are your secret weapon.

THE VALUE OF VALUES

Have you ever stopped to think about what you, personally, value? Every person has a unique set of things that they believe. Most of us learned our values young, from our families and caregivers through a process called *imprinting*. As you became an adult and gained more life experience, your values matured. Influenced by friends, culture, and your own ideas, they developed into the most important, defining part of your personality, and what sets you apart as a unique human being. They attracted you to certain relationships and pushed you away from others.

Whether you were conscious of it or not, your values drove every decision you made in your life—from who you chose as soul mate, to your education, to where you live and where you work, what employees you hire and what clients you attract. Researchers will say that even what team you root for is a reflection of what matters to you.

What about your business? Whether you're the founder, a senior leader, or a middle manager, can you articulate what the company you dedicate so much time to values? Can you point to the things that make you different?

Just like people, every organization has values, and a core set of goals and beliefs that influence its strategy and direction. Businesses are founded with the values and priorities of their earliest leaders. Those can change and evolve over time, especially during periods of major transition, succession, or intentional review.

Value statements aren't always articulated, but they always exist. And they don't always match what's printed on the letterhead (or, these days, in the

51

company's official email signature).

If you show me where a company invests its time and resources, I'll show you what it values. When I was young, I had a teacher who always reminded her classes that "actions speak louder than words." And that's still true. An individual or a business' true values are a reflection of what *others* see in their behavior every day. If you pay attention to your own business—how it's run, what leaders talk about, what it measures, how it makes decisions—you can see the different preferences and priorities shining through.

And if you consider those values and how they relate to the question of trust, you'll also be able to see a business' future. As Joey Reiman, an incredibly talented brand consultant, puts it, "Values are to business what religion is to culture; they give soul to an otherwise mechanical process to make profit. Without them, we make poor money."

It's important to point out here that values are deeply personal, and can't be measured or defined in relation to your competitors or acquaintances. Living a values-driven life, or leading a values-driven organization, is about being the best, most authentic version of yourself, regardless of outside influences. There's an enormous freedom in that, because it means that embracing your values means letting go of the dangerous comparison traps that often drag us away from what truly drives us. When we no longer worry about how our choices measure up to others, or "what will they think of me?" we're free to be ourselves.

Not long ago, I had the privilege to work with a company that exemplified to me what shared values could look like. We'd been approached by the California Avocado Commission, a professional network of more than 5,000 small farmers and growers across the state. They had never spent much time or money on advertising before, but now they wanted a fresh way to distinguish themselves from their competition, mostly imported from Mexico and South America.

From an advertising perspective, it's hard to differentiate a fruit. Whether it's Chilean or American, an avocado is green, bumpy, and it tastes good. The message to consumers needed to go deeper than the product and into the values that made the people who grow California avocados stand out to customers. And so in our first meeting together, our team asked the Commission to describe what was important to their members. Their answer was inspired. Instead of going into a long explanation of a farmer's experience and the best way to grow an avocado, the Commission invited us to come and see for ourselves. And what we discovered was extraordinary.

The fields were beautiful, and the people who grew them were passionate about their work. Avocados are not a crop that can be mass produced or mechanically harvested. So it's small, local, independent farmers, working anywhere from five to five hundred acres, who thrive with hard work and patience.

I'll never forget one particular story. The farmer had worked in corporate banking for years but left mid-career to try his hand at avocados. He said, "I love giving people a piece of California sunshine—that's what avocados are to me. I can stand at the top of my orchard at the end of the day, and look at the sun setting over the ocean, and I think that God could have put me in no better spot in my life. I can't imagine ever doing anything else."

How could a potential customer *not* react to a person who so clearly had his values and purpose figured out?

No one had ever sat down and asked the independent California farmers to articulate their values, and they didn't spend a lot of time trying to tell me why their avocados were worth more than the competition's, but their culture was so rooted (pardon the pun) in what was truly important to them, and what brought them joy, that we saw it as soon as we looked.

The California farmers produced a high-quality product, setting and maintaining standards of production that were above bare government compliance. They worked out of a respect for the land and the legacy. Most of these farms were passed through generations and were run by families working together. Over and over, farmers told us that no one chooses avocado farming to get rich. They were all here for something else. I heard stories like, "Yeah we were tempted to sell out and take the easy way. We could be sitting on some beach somewhere, probably in Mexico, retired. But this is our life, and this is what we do. We wouldn't trade it for anything."

The values were there. Our job became to connect customers with that story, and with the real people who were part of bringing their food to them. We took cameras to the farms and introduced California avocado farmers to the world: the father and son team of Duncan and Robert; Gene, the former math teacher; Mark and Linda, who are raising two children on their farm; and dozens of other unique, individual stories of the hands that grow California avocados.

Our first television spot opened with the line, "Avocados aren't in the hand of Mother Nature. They're in the hands of a guy named Carl." The growers loved it, because we were highlighting them and the hard work they put into their craft. The customers loved it, because it made their food purchase personal.

Sales skyrocketed to an all-time high. "Hand grown in California" avocados earned a 90% preference among American shoppers to avocados grown anywhere else in the world. Shoppers demonstrated that they were willing to pay a premium for something that was of the highest quality, and that was healthy for everyone: the purchaser, the farmer, and the environment.

The future belongs to the California Avocado Commission, and others like it, who see themselves as part of something bigger than the transaction and the bottom line.

BENEFITS OF A VALUES-DRIVEN LIFE

Without guiding principles beyond the base desires for power, prestige, position, pleasure, and profit, businesses stagnate internally, even as they may appear successful. Leaders feel it. Employees feel it. And even if they don't understand it, in this global world of transparent communication, customers end up feeling it, too. There's a lack of engagement that comes from a lack of purpose.

Living a life of shared values—both as an individual and as a brand—builds long-term trust, loyalty, and relationships. Why? Because values offer unparalleled benefits.

They provide purpose. My father was a career military man in the Greatest Generation, and a Nightfighter pilot in World War II. He was a squadron leader at twenty-two. He was shot down three times, and was one of the first forces to occupy Japan. Every day he had to make life-and-death decisions, and he needed to convince a group of other men to do the same. One of the most important leadership lessons he ever taught me was that the way to motivate soldiers wasn't to tell them *where* they were fighting. It was to tell them *why* they were fighting.

55

Shared values are a more valuable tool than any business plan or ad campaign you'll ever launch, because they are what give your community the *why*. Men going into battle didn't care about the field strategy or the battle plan unless they'd already accepted the cause and the reason they were putting their lives on the line. As the leader, it was his responsibility to remind his men of the shared *purpose*.

One of the first questions we ask our clients now is this: Does your company have an articulated *why*? Is it the driving force behind the strategic decisions you make, and the motivator that gives employees purpose? Understanding the size of their *why* lets us see the amount of risk they're willing to take, the number of attacks they can survive, and the effort they're able to muster.

Without the *why* that's bigger than a paycheck, it's easy to give up when trials test a company's resolve. Many workplaces try to make do with a business plan that focuses only on short-term goals and often meaningless, transactional measurements. In these places, our research shows that job satisfaction and engagement plummet. Workers report that their days are spent going in circles, dragging themselves through meaningless meetings that seem to have no purpose other than taking them away from the parts of their job they truly enjoy. Or worse, frustrated employees are left to interpret the company's *why* for themselves, and often come to the conclusion that the values of the distant, mysterious leadership are in direct conflict with their own. Without purpose, they're left with no goal other than escaping to a competitor or, often, to leave the business world all together.

They guide us. I've read that if you set out from the equator to circumnavigate the globe, if your setting is just one degree off, you'll miss your destination by five hundred miles. Professing values and living them out are very different propositions. But when we are authentic, our values are our "True North" when making tough decisions. Without them, our plans can miss the mark significantly.

I make multiple choices every day, from what to eat to sensitive decisions about staffing to how to communicate with my wife. Sometimes the onslaught of choices becomes dizzying. However, when I allow my values to chart my course, those choices become much easier to make. Values provide my ethical and moral framework through which I can identify the *right* thing vs. the *expedient* thing.

In the early years of running our agency, this principle was put to the test. We had a lucrative contract with a well-known client, but their CMO was, to put it softly, a difficult person. He was abrasive and arrogant, and he abused our staff. Knowing how to handle it wasn't an easy decision, and it was one of my own early lessons in leadership. My partners and I struggled with what to do, and we hesitated for a long time, hoping that the situation would correct itself. We loved the work we were producing for them, and we needed the revenue. Yet I could feel the tension in our office, spreading like a cancer. In the end we realized that maintaining a relationship for the income it produced was contrary to our values. For the sake of the talented and dedicated people who worked for me, I had one of the most awkward meetings of my career and "fired" the client.

Planting the flag of our values may seem like a monumental act, and in many ways it is, but using those values to take action cements the bond between word and deed. Firing that client cost us in the short term through lack of revenue. But what we gained in employee trust and dedication more than offset the loss.

Establishing and communicating a brand's values allows multiple individuals to share that same "True North" certainty. When faced with a choice, they have a compass of the company's values to guide them. Each year, according to a 2015 article in *The Washington Post*, almost half of American employees witness "unethical or illegal" behaviors in their workplaces. Yet shortcuts and bending the rules doesn't pay off in the long term: the stock price growth of the companies ranked with the "most ethical cultures" outperformed all other stock market and peer measures by almost 300%.[29]

When you're a leader, all eyes are on you. Every move is scrutinized, and every decision is measured. If employees see that the values that drive you are "profit at all cost," then their default decisions may not be "work with integrity." Healthy, positive corporate values protect a business' long-term potential by setting expectations for employee behavior and governing poor choices. They give employees better tools to resist pressure to perform harmful actions and increase the likelihood of an organization's overall ethical behavior.

They distinguish us. In this new, over-commoditized marketplace, your values are the new corporate currency. Chances are that there are a dozen or more companies that provide the same product or service that you do. Your customers have choices. Values form the life raft that helps you float above the sea of sameness.

Southern California is full of healthy food and beverage outlets, both well-promoted chains and exclusive, expensive boutiques. So when a new juice franchiser called Nekter approached us for help, one of our first conversations had to be about what would distinguish them. What we heard intrigued us.

According to the thoughtful, passionate owners of Nekter, there are plenty of brands already touting their organic concoctions and reaching the affluent market that can afford twelve dollar drinks. But there are huge markets where healthy, convenient juices are still hard to find. Nekter's primary value is to make a healthy lifestyle available and affordable to everyone. To accomplish this, they source fresh, local produce from reliable sources and have plans to partner with schools and urban gardens, regardless of whether those locales carry the coveted "certified organic" label. By sacrificing one commoditized label, they distinguish the story that truly sets them apart.

Your collection of priorities and beliefs are the ingredients that make you unique. How you express them sets you apart as an individual with a greater purpose than just the next sale, and attracts the customers who share your values. People don't buy what you do; people buy why you do it.

They engage us. It's hard to motivate employees—or ourselves, for that matter—when the only goal is increasing the bottom line. Money—even in the form of growing personal salaries—just doesn't drive us to care. But values draw us into a shared higher purpose. The numbers back me up here. A 2007 Towers Perrin survey reported that companies with high levels of employee engagement reported a 19% increase in operating income and a 28% increase in earnings growth. However, low-level engagement led to a 33% decrease in operating income and an 11% annual decline in earnings.[30] Sharing a vision builds employee loyalty and focuses everyone on bigger goals. Blake Mycoskie, founder of the multi-million dollar company TOMS Shoes, is often quoted as saying "The greatest competitive advantage is to allow your employees to be a part of something. Something bigger than what you're doing." We'll look at the values of Mycoskie and TOMS more in the following chapter.

Perhaps no well-known brand lives this out better than the Apple Store. The retailer takes in more money per square foot than any other brand, and its employees are widely recognized as some of the most enthusiastic, supportive service workers in the United States. How does it do it? There are probably a number of factors, but we can't overlook the importance of the training and communication the company offers its front-line staff. A reporter for *The New York Times* describes it as "an employee culture that tries to turn every job into an exalted mission."[31] Apple Store workers aren't just there to fix an iPhone or sell a new laptop; their real purpose is to "enrich people's lives." One former store manager told the reporter that Apple was a place that "wanted you to be the best you could be in life, not just in sales."

I've been in hundreds of corporate headquarters, and I can tell you that when there's a shared sense of purpose even the air feels different, compared to businesses where there's chaos and dysfunction. Values give us something to work toward together.

They bond us. Values drive a deep emotional connection between company and customer, and between employer and employee. For decades, the fast food chain Chick-fil-A has drawn controversy and attention for its policy to keep all of its franchises and stores closed on Sundays as an expression of their values. Plenty of people are suspicious. How could they compete, financially, with chains that were open seven days a week? Every Sunday, they run the risk that Chick-fil-A customers will be tempted to go somewhere else. What if they never come back? Yet the company that touts itself as "the largest quick-service chicken restaurant chain in the country" continues to grow, with system-wide annual sales of $5 billion.[32] They even outperform every other American fast food restaurant, including McDonalds, in store-over-store revenue.[33] For every customer that they might lose for their decision, another is drawn to them specifically because of their commitment to give their employees a day of rest. In fact, Chick-fil-A customers are so loyal that they'll camp out in pup tents when a new store opens in order to be part of the "First100" customers. Rain, snow, dark of night...your local mail carrier has nothing on the bond that these customers have with the brand.

Outdoor retailer REI has its own loyal, connected base of customers. As a co-op, the national retailer invests up to 80% of its profits back to its 5.5 million members in the form of dividends. But that's not what keeps customers coming back for backpacks, kayaks, and mountain bikes, or what keeps its skilled staff of outdoor experts enthusiastic about planning trips, sizing gear, and helping customers day after day. What bonds REI members and customers is a passionate love of going outside.

Two of REI's publicly shared values are *"authenticity: being true to the outdoors"* and *"balance: encouraging each other to enjoy all aspects of life."* Their shared commitment to preserving nature has brought REI's CEO, Jerry Strizke, its employees, and its connected customers to parks and wilderness areas several times a year to work, side by side, on conservation projects. But in 2015 REI took their commitment to the outdoors, and to their stakeholders, to a whole new level by announcing that instead of following the trend of opening earlier and selling more stuff on Black Friday, it would *close* all 143 of its stores, as well as its warehouses, on the day after Thanksgiving. REI gave all 12,000 of its employees a paid day off to "go outside." Strizke explained their process this way:

"We believe that being outside makes our lives better. And Black Friday is the perfect time to remind ourselves of this essential truth. We're a different kind of company—and while the rest of the world is fighting it out in the aisles, we'll be spending our day a little differently. We're choosing to opt outside, and want you to come with us."[34]

That kind of invitation drew an overwhelmingly positive response and tightened the bond that already existed between REI and its stakeholders. One store manager described the response to the initial announcement as "hugging and hollering. For five sustained minutes, everyone was just cheering and clapping."[35] When the company shared their plans with the public, the #OptOutside hashtag took off across the Internet, with almost 300,000 signing up for the campaign in the first two days,[36] and social media flooded with customers sharing their own plans to forgo the post-turkey consumer frenzy and spend time with family—and then come back to do their holiday shopping at REI.

Those shared values, more than the bottom line or a love of the product itself, lead to satisfaction, loyalty, and trust. Companies also receive grace when they stumble, an idea we'll go into in more detail in Chapter 9.

They transport us. Out of all of the benefits of living out our values, this is the most important. Our shared values are the key to the gate that leads to deep, identification-based trust, the most valuable corporate asset you can accrue. We cannot have that true sense of intimacy with another person, or a sense of deeply knowing that a brand reflects a piece of ourselves, without sharing values. Your values cannot be replicated. Competitors can add more features and underprice you, but they cannot disrupt the trust you build with your employees and customers. Values take us on a journey toward a higher purpose.

As author Simon Simek said in a popular TEDx talk, "The goal is not just to sell to people who need what you have; the goal is to sell to people who believe what you believe. The goal is not just to hire people who need a job; it's to hire people who believe what you believe."[37]

Now, before we get carried away on a cloud of happy feelings and bright promises, let me remind you: it's not an easy journey. Trust isn't built on a "love at first sight" fairy tale, and customers don't flock to build loyal brand relationships after the first ad campaign. It takes time, integrity, and, yes, consistency. But the payoff is enormous. Shared values in a business setting can form the foundation of a tribe of loyal, committed followers who will intertwine their own identity with the brand, and will be a lifetime ambassador and supporter.

Just ask Howard Shultz.

THE RISK OF VALUES

So if values reveal what we really believe and help us stand out from the sea of sameness, why aren't more organizations flying their values flags?

Because living a life of values is not without risk. Values can be like magnets: they attract plenty of attention, but they'll also repel certain incompatible forces. In today's polarized culture, making a stand is putting a target on your head, and leaving it visible for someone else to cajole or attack.

When Tim Cook became the CEO of Apple in 2011—stepping into the role previously held by the legendary creative genius Steve Jobs—customers, employees, and investors held their collective breath. Apple had foundered before when Jobs wasn't in control. Cook was a virtual unknown, a man who'd been keeping a low profile in operations for years. The rumors started. The jackals were ready to pounce. In The Values Institute's Most Trustworthy

Brands survey that year, the company slipped in its trust-based ranking for the first (and only) time.

But Apple had something going for it, and Tim Cook was smart enough to know that. The brand has some of the strongest, clearest values of any company in the modern world, and they were working. "We value originality and innovation and pour our lives into making the best products on earth," Cook said in his first letter to his employees. "Steve built a company and culture that is unlike any other in the world and we are going to stay true to that—it is in our DNA."

Cook kept Apple on a consistent path. He expanded markets, and patiently, in time, released new products. But he also planted his own flag by highlighting some of the previously understated Apple values and extending the well-known focus on innovation to include an investment in environmental responsibility. "Innovation means working with what's here to create something new," according to the company website, which goes on to highlight micro-hydro projects and solar farms to generate renewable energy.[38]

That philosophy came under attack at an annual shareholder meeting, when Cook outlined several new initiatives to cut Apple's environmental footprint. Reportedly, one of the shareholders stood up and publicly urged Cook and Apple's board of directors not to pursue environmental initiatives that don't contribute to the company's bottom line.

Cook's response was atypically sharp. "We do things because they are right and just, and that is who we are. That's who we are as a company," he reportedly replied. "When I think about human rights, I don't think about an ROI. When I think about making our products accessible for the people that can't see or to help a kid with autism, I don't think about a bloody ROI, and by the same token, I don't think about helping our environment from an ROI point of view."[39]

The shareholder sat down. Apple went on to show a year-over-year decline in its carbon footprint for the first time since it started tracking its environmental impact.

Taking a stand like that, especially against those who have power, requires courage. And after the last ten years of economic and global insecurity, many of the leaders I talk to are deeply risk averse, or are working in companies that feel risk averse. When we've lived until now thinking that the ultimate goal is to build power, prestige, position, pleasure, and especially profit, doing something that could cost even a piece of those can seem dangerous.

The real risk in a Values Economy isn't planting your flag and living by your values. The risk happens when you don't take a stand for anything, and therefore don't distinguish yourself. Then you become wallpaper, and the world moves right past you. You've lost your magnet, and your customers and employees are at risk of slipping away.

I once read a biblical commentary about the passage in the book of Revelation that says, "I know your deeds, that you are neither cold nor hot. I wish you were either one or the other!" It explained that there's no real value in lukewarm water. Cold water is refreshing. It has medicinal purposes in wound care and relieving swelling. And hot water relaxes muscles, regulates body temperature, and sterilizes. But lukewarm water is neither medicinal, nor does it feel good. It's not refreshing. It's not stimulating. It's just there.

The individuals and organizations who are afraid of their own values are sitting in lukewarm water. They have no purpose.

Is this all there is?

Not if you don't want it to be.

GET READY FOR THE LONG HAUL

As I talk to leaders about values, I'm often reminded of the Greek proverb that says, "A society grows great when old men plant trees whose shade they know they shall never sit in." The opportunity to live and work in a culture based on values is an investment in redefining success and contributing to something that lasts long beyond our own tenure.

Human beings want to be engaged, and to feel a shared sense of purpose— not just with our closest loved ones, but with anyone, and any group, within our circle of trust. We want to believe that a person is interested in us for our own sake, and not simply for what they can take from us. And when we have so many different options and opportunities, we want to believe that a brand cares about more than our money. We want to believe that they care about the same things we do.

The Values Economy has replaced the Transaction Economy, and it's thriving, driven not by the immediate gratification of the next quarterly report, but by the long-term ideas and goals that drive you and connect you to your customers, and that provide you with a purpose that's bigger than the bottom line. The currency is trust, earned through consistent, creative, and faithful application of your values, both within your walls and with your customers. In the next chapter, we'll take a deeper look at what that looks like.

But I want to make this clear: positioning yourself and your company to be better aligned with your customers' values is not a quick fix. This isn't as easy as developing a new caption for an ad campaign. It's a fundamental shift.

If you approach it without authenticity—as a way to acquire more profit or position or power—the hypocrisy will reveal itself and you will fail.

In 2000, Howard Schultz stepped down as the CEO of Starbucks Coffee Company. Although he remained the chairman, the company hit bumps. In Shultz's opinion, they lost sight of the values that had held them together and set them apart. The Starbucks reputation took a hit. The stock price plummeted.

Eight years later, Schultz returned to the helm to right the ship. He didn't do it because he needed the money; he's already one of the richest men in the country. But as he said in one interview, "What I stand for is not just to make money; it's to preserve the integrity of what we have built for 39 years—to look in the mirror and feel like I've done something that has meaning and relevancy and is something people are going to respect. You have to be willing to fight for what you believe in."[40]

That's the Values Economy.

FOUR

CHARACTERISTICS OF A VALUES-DRIVEN COMPANY

Once I've introduced the Values Economy and made the case for the importance of focusing on shared values as the foundation of trust, business leaders often ask me for a list of the "right" values that will ensure success. After all, everyone ascribes to some values, but not everyone finds the personal satisfaction of a Howard Schultz or the corporate success of a Starbucks Coffee Company. Busy executives, understandably, want to know how to find that path to sustainability and success, and how to avoid the fate of so many businesses that crumble in failure.

So their questions make sense:

Is there a secret list of values that will bring satisfaction and success?

Are there values that are better for a particular business than others?

Unfortunately, no. We've studied hundreds of companies, and have concluded that it's not that easy. You can't pull a list of values off the shelf and plug it in like it was a product in an electronics store. Values are unique to a culture, and they must come from the hearts and minds of those who are responsible for your business and your customers on a daily basis. Your values will not, and should not, look the same as anyone else's.

And yet, like the famous Supreme Court ruling, when it comes to values-driven companies, employees and customers "know it when we see it." We are naturally drawn to certain companies, and certain messages, while others fail to elicit a single spark.

What's the difference?

Let me start by telling you about a company that definitely *didn't* have it.

A few years ago, our agency was invited to meet with a potential client in the financial industry and share a basic "capabilities" presentation. The company's president had been warm and affable on the phone, and there were about twenty people in the board room when we started.

About fifteen minutes into my talk, I was explaining our agency's commitment to identifying and sharing a company's values when the door swung open and a man walked in. He had a swagger and a gold chain around his neck. This was some sort of alpha dog, and his presence had an immediate effect.

It was as if the air had been sucked out of the room. Twenty pairs of eyes were suddenly studying the table or the carpet. No one was breathing.

"Don't start over for me," the late arrival announced as he swung himself into a chair next to a terrified-looking intern. "I'm just the CEO."

Ah. I nodded to him, but before I could pick up the presentation, he interrupted again. "What have you got for me?"

No one in the room, not even the president, was looking at me. I'd been abandoned to the shark. I explained that we were giving a capabilities presentation, and that we were talking about the importance of shared values.

"What the hell do values have to do with anything?" he barked. "What are values going to get me?"

I stepped back into the presentation and shared, briefly, how values help businesses succeed. The CEO was not impressed.

"Okay," he said, his voice absolutely dripping with disdain. "I'll play your game. I'll tell you what I *value*. I value money. That's what you're here to make more of for me. In fact, I value money so much that if I could spread it out on my bed and sleep in it every night, I would. And if you can help me do that, you're hired. So let's stop talking about *values*. Where are your ideas? Where are your pitches? You're an ad agency. Sell me something."

By this point, my agency partner, Mark, was kicking me under the table, although it wasn't clear whether he was trying to goad me or warn me not to engage. Either way, I knew this conversation was over. I gathered my papers and closed my laptop. "I appreciate your honesty," I told him. "And all I can say is that I hope you're happy with your money, and I hope you sleep well with it. There's apparently not much we can do to help you."

The CEO was unperturbed by his effect. Before he sauntered back out of the room he looked at the president, who had invited us in the first place, and sneered. "This was a colossal waste of time."

When the door closed behind him, everyone around the table took what felt like their first breath in minutes.

"Well, that went pretty well," the CMO finally offered. "You got him to talk about values."

I shook my head. "Let me guess. He sets the culture around here?" I waited until a few heads timidly nodded. "Then I am really sorry. I'm sorry for you all. But there aren't values here that we share. There's nothing we can do to help."

It was hard to walk away from that company, hard to leave an executive team and marketing staff who seemed engaged and eager for change. But a company's leaders drive its culture, and their values influence its decisions. If this company existed for the sole purpose of filling a man's sheets with money, there wasn't much hope for building trust with his customers.

TWO TYPES OF VALUES

In general, a company's identified values can be split into two different types: **compliant values** and **influential values**.

Compliant values are the generic, lifeless, non-distinguishing words that exist on paper, but don't actually affect the day-to-day. Most transaction-driven companies have a list of values on their website in order to look good while they pursue their own self interests however they see fit. You've heard them—they're words like *excellence, success, quality,* or *service.* They sound good, but what do they actually change?

Compliant values are safe to post on the break room wall, because they can't be measured. Employees and customers can't identify how compliant values affect business decisions.

On the other hand, influential values cast their shadow on every element of a workplace. Influential values are words that come from the hearts of the people in your company. These are true ideals that take a stand, plant a flag, and tattoo themselves across the face of an organization. Instead of reflecting the same words that everyone else uses, they're measurable, and often are somewhat counter-cultural.

71

One of the values of the Disneyland theme park is *Magical Moments*. Every employee, from the janitor to the guy in the Aladdin suit, is trained that their primary job is to offer every guest not just a pleasant experience, but a magical one. The Internet is full of stories of cast members going above and beyond what would be considered customer service in order to truly make each guest's experience full of unexpected delight.

Not far away from Disneyland, at St. Joseph Hospital in Orange, California, the value that guides employees on a day-to-day basis is *Sacred Encounters*. Every interaction with patients, visitors, and fellow staff members is a chance to make a connection, to bring peace and support to someone who's often facing a difficult situation. They are committed to being aware of the possibility of each moment, whether that looks like a nurse stopping in a busy shift to assure the parents of a pediatric patient that "we'll take care of your child," or a graveyard-shift cafeteria worker offering a hug to a tired resident.

Influential values like this bring accountability, because you can see and measure how they are applied. *Would a proposed change in the budget or staffing affect our commitment to Sacred Encounters? Will this potential job candidate offer Magical Moments?* Influential values never fade into the website wallpaper, and customers see that.

A person or a brand that takes the risk in order to stand for something that matters, and something that will actually affect day-to-day decisions and investments, will be rewarded with trust and long-term sustainability. Influential values distinguish your company from all competitors, draw a loyal community of dedicated followers, and can change the way people view your brand and your category.

How do you know if your values are compliant or influential? Sometimes it's as easy as looking at the words. If you don't know what they mean or why they matter, or can't point to specific examples of how they affect your everyday business, chances are that they are compliant. If the values are ideas that you return to when you need to make important decisions, then they are influential.

FIVE CHARACTERISTICS OF A VALUE-DRIVEN BUSINESS

Not every influential value, though, has the same effect. After all, the Five Ps that we looked at earlier in the book— power, position, prestige, pleasure, and prosperity—are easily measurable, and can influence businesses to take certain actions every day.

And so even for businesses that demonstrate influential values, we must ask a second question: *where does it lead?*

In the Bible, the Apostle Paul seems to have been wrestling with the same ideas when he wrote to the Roman citizens of Corinth:

"'I have the right to do anything,' you say—but not everything is beneficial. 'I have the right to do anything'—but not everything is constructive."

According to our research, what's most important isn't the word that a business chooses to describe its value, but the way that it expresses it to the community of employees and customers, who evaluate a company's values and priorities based on two simple questions:

Does this value exist to benefit others, or to hurt others?

Does this value build trust?

Over the past decade of research, The Values Institute has identified five specific characteristics that distinguish the businesses with influential, beneficial values that attract customers and build relationships. The companies we've studied that are thriving in the Values Economy demonstrate all five of these elements in the ways that they communicate both internally and externally.

For each characteristic, I'll give you a question or two to help you take stock of where you are right now. But then we'll also dig into some case studies. In our experience working with business leaders, since values are something that we feel, and some words have different meanings for different people, it helps to study well-known cases and examples of what values look like in familiar stories. Most of the following examples look at national or international brands and well-publicized situations, but these principles work whether there are five people in your business or five hundred thousand, and whether you're all in a one-room workshop or are scattered all over the globe.

RELATIONSHIP VS. TRANSACTION

Do you see your customers as people or account numbers? Does your senior leadership respect the employees, and treat them as collaborators who make significant contributions?

Companies that thrive in the Values Economy are intentional about building long-term loyalty instead of chasing the quick sale. A relationship is not something you can decide to add, or subtract, like an item in a grocery cart. It doesn't happen with a number on a screen. As we've established already, a relationship is a framework that is built over time, and because of mutual desire. It's a choice, and an investment.

A relationship between a brand and a customer, or a brand and an employee, lasts longer than the moment it takes to exchange goods for services, or the time it takes to earn a paycheck. It's based on always considering the humanity of the person on the other end of the equation, and of considering their needs and not just what you can sell them.

That kind of investment takes time, but the long-term rewards are worth it. Committing to relationships ensures that you will save money on customer acquisition costs and HR headaches in the future. It's far easier to serve a repeat customer and work with a valued employee than to constantly invest money and time into chasing someone new. And on the more intangible side, developing relationships creates a culture that engages our common humanity and encourages our trust and deeper connections. When we have a genuine relationship with someone, we see them as something more than a cost or a profit.

This is something that the online shoe retailer Zappos knows intrinsically. There is perhaps no company in the world that has the same laser-focused commitment to its customers. The founder of Zappos, Tony Hsieh, literally wrote the book on providing great service and called it *Delivering Happiness*. The Zappos website announces that their "Core Value #1" is to "deliver WOW through service."

What does that mean?

To WOW, you must differentiate yourself, which means doing something a little unconventional and innovative. You must do something that's above and beyond what's expected. And whatever you do must have an emotional impact on the receiver. We are not an average company, our service is not average, and we don't want our people to be average. We expect every employee to deliver WOW.

Whether internally with co-workers or externally with our customers and partners, delivering WOW results in word of mouth. Our philosophy at Zappos is to WOW with service and experience, not with anything that relates directly to monetary compensation (for example, we don't offer blanket discounts or promotions to customers).[41]

In practice, Zappos' values are on full display in every aspect of their interaction with customers. But perhaps their best-known example is the ten-hour customer service phone call.

Bestselling author and business expert Peter Drucker says, "What's measured improves." While most transaction-based companies train their phone and online customer service employees to stick to a script and get customers off the phone as fast as possible, and some even measure employee success by a call duration metric, Zappos tells its "customer loyalty team members" to take as much time as the customer needs, and gives them wide latitude to meet each person's unique needs. Zappos measures things like, *Did the agent try to make a personal emotional connection? Did they keep the rapport going after the customer responded to their attempt? Did they address unstated needs? Did they provide a "wow experience"?*

In one particular case, a college student in the Midwest had questions about shoe options—but then the conversation shifted to the customer's upcoming move to Las Vegas, where Zappos is headquartered. It didn't matter that the call happened in early December, the busiest season for retailers. The Zappos representative stayed on the phone as long as the customer wanted, offering advice about neighborhoods and what to pack—for *ten hours and twenty-nine minutes*. The customer eventually ordered one pair of shoes, but, to Zappos, that wasn't the point. The relationship was.

Joseph Mitchell, the author of *The Zappos Experience*, says "Zappos invests in the call center not as cost, but the opportunity to market."[42] The result? As many as 75% of purchases on Zappos.com come from returning customers, who order 2.5 times more than a first-time buyer.

And Zappos doesn't just build relationships with its customers. Employees, too, are treated as valued individuals. Call-center employees have full autonomy to meet needs in the best ways possible—even if it means finding a product from another retailer, purchasing it, and hand-delivering it.

Another one of the Family Core Values is "create fun and a little weirdness." As Zappos describes it, "We don't want to become one of those big companies that feels corporate and boring. We want to be able to laugh at ourselves. We look for both fun and humor in our daily work." They demonstrate this among their teams by encouraging creativity in dress and personal space design. Employees are encouraged to mingle and get to know other staff members, and to be, as Hsieh says, "the same person at home and at the office." To encourage departmental mixing and personal development, they have organized job shadowing programs—bringing together employees with different job responsibilities to share work time and teach one another about their roles— and encourage employees to explore their interests. Every quarter, Zappos hosts an all-hands company meeting, where along with the regular company news and updates, employees showcase their personal talents, from bands to dancing to improv acts.

Those relationships have built a successful empire, which is consistently ranked as one of *Fortune Magazine*'s Top 100 Companies to work for, but also regularly tops $1 billion in annual sales.

Despite examples like this, and all of the evidence that shows that relationships enhance business and personal experiences, many companies still get stuck on the quick sale and the fast buck. They charge as much as they can, and deliver as little as possible. They'll trample their relationships in order to pad their bottom line. They demand that employees to follow policy, not work with people.

Perhaps no case demonstrates this transaction value more than the battle that grieving families face with cell phone companies after the death of a loved one. When Darrel Daziel passed away in San Francisco in 2012, his family called his cell phone carrier, T-Mobile, to cancel the account. The call center worker said the account could not be canceled until the family provided a copy of the death certificate. In order to waive an "early termination fee," that form had to be sent within thirty days of the customer's passing—and no, the rep could not make exceptions or offer compassion for families dealing with far more pressing issues of loss. Even after the certificate was delivered, T-Mobile continued to send bills while Darrel's phone lay, unused, in a drawer. Darrel's son called to complain, but call center workers claimed that they weren't authorized to change or cancel a plan, for any reason. When the family refused to pay, the carrier turned the statement over to a collections agency, which harassed the deceased man's widow. It was only when the family went to the media, which drew attention to T-Mobile's bad behavior, that a public relations spokesperson apologized and claimed "This was an isolated incident."[43]

Except it wasn't. Reports continued to surface of similar problems all around the world. The family of a twenty-four-year-old woman tragically killed in a motorcycle crash was already crushed under reams of medical bills and paperwork when they realized T-Mobile was still billing the dead woman's account. The carrier claimed the family sent the death certificate to the wrong address, and so therefore owed money for the months since her death. They even refused to waive the termination fee.[44] Two years later, a frustrated widow in Wales brought her husband's ashes to the local T-Mobile store when the provider not only refused to cancel her husband's account, but regularly texted to offer him upgrade packages.[45] And lest it seem like I'm picking on T-Mobile, there are similar heartless stories for most of the major American carriers.

In the age of social media, stories like this get out. A single bad transaction tarnishes not only the relationship with the affected customer, but the overall reputation of a company. Companies and individuals that tread on others in their rush for revenue may end up with more money in the cash register, but it happens at the expense of their long-term ability for growth. Disgruntled customers share their experiences. They look for other alternatives. And the transaction-driven company is stuck trying to attract new customers.

People have options today. One of the benefits of the commoditized marketplace is that there are plenty of other choices. We don't need to stay in relationships that are abusive or neglectful. If we don't trust you, we can choose not to work with you.

Purpose Before Profit

Why are you in the business you're in? Are you inviting your customers and employees to be part of something that's bigger than a transaction? One hundred years from now, what do you want people to remember about your business?

Your values are demonstrated, often, by your company's story, and its reason for being. As we've seen in previous chapters, a company builds trust and relationships by connecting with others through shared values, and demonstrating a reason to exist that lasts longer than the bottom line. In a time when consumers have almost limitless choices, trust and loyalty are built by inviting them to join you for something more substantial than commerce.

Note that I'm not saying "*instead of*" the bottom line. There's a reason that this is purpose *before* profit, and not *vs.* It's not an either/or situation. I want to be clear about this, because I'm also a business owner with a mortgage to pay and a payroll to meet. Choosing to live a life of values doesn't mean that you have to ignore the bottom line. There's nothing wrong with having a healthy profit margin and being financially successful. Customers and employees generally understand that a company needs to make money in order to sustain itself and grow. But they do have a problem with companies that make a profit without a purpose.

If a company exists only to make themselves richer at the expense of others, then there's nowhere for employees and customers to meet with shared values. However, with a greater sense of purpose, even profit takes on a new shine. Employees who feel emotionally connected to a vision that transcends revenue are healthier, happier, and more collaborative. Customers, in turn, reward companies whose values align with their own with loyalty and advocacy. They align with businesses that invite them to be a part of a greater mission.

In 2002, a young, energetic serial entrepreneur was looking for his next big idea. As Blake Mycoskie traveled off the beaten tourist paths of Argentina, he was horrified by the poverty he discovered. Specifically, what tugged his heart were the children who didn't have money for shoes.

And so the "One for One" purpose was born: Mycoskie decided to create a shoe company for wealthier first-world shoppers, but it came with a unique catch: for every pair of shoes they sold, the company would give a second pair to a child who needed them.

Can you imagine an employee going to their classic, transaction-based supervisor with a scheme like that? They're giving away half their products! But Mycoskie didn't ask anyone's permission. And it was a compelling story for customers and his early employees. This wasn't about indulging in over-consumption or selling someone another pair of shoes they don't need. This was about building a community of people to help give shoes to those who didn't have any. There was a clear, emotional reason for customers to build loyalty with this company over its competitors. TOMS grew quickly, achieving 10 million sales (and, therefore, 10 million donations) in ten years. It's expanded the "one to one" model to other areas, as well, like TOMS Eyewear and TOMS Coffee, which use proceeds from the sale of coffee beans and designer sunglasses to fund eye surgeries and clean water programs.

Do your customers and employees know why you do the business that you do? Do you communicate a goal beyond your own profit? Purposes grow as they're shared, but they can also become tangled if you're not honest about your real motivations. Customers and employees aren't easily fooled—and when they've been burned, the punishment can be brutal. That's something that another shoe company, Skechers, learned.

In 2009, the company released a new line of athletic shoes—the Shape-Ups, Tone-Ups, and Resistance Runners. The ad campaigns for the awkward-looking, rocker-bottom shoes with the curved bottoms promised that customers could "get in shape without setting foot in a gym." The purpose of the shoes, the company touted, was to help people lose weight, tone lower body muscles, and even combat heart disease. Many customers bought in, believing that Skechers was acting for the purpose of improving the health and wellbeing of their customers.

Only, of course, no pair of shoes can really live up to those claims. When customers didn't see the results they were promised, they filed class action suits. The Federal Trade Commission determined that the studies that Skechers cited in their commercials were bogus or misstated. The company ended up paying a $40 million settlement, and had to promise not to make further unsubstantiated claims about its shoes. Their real purpose—selling more shoes—was painfully clear.

If you give your employees and customers a story, they will share it. If it's bigger than the bottom line, it will draw others.

Transparency vs. Opacity

How much are you openly and honestly sharing with your colleagues, employees, and customers about your business decisions? When things are difficult, do you resort to partial truths and PR spin?

Most of you who have personal relationships with a spouse, a child, or a friend know that honest, authentic communication is the backbone of trust. My wife would be understandably upset if I made major decisions about our lives without talking to her about them—or, worse, lying to her about it, even by omission. My business partners would be justifiably concerned if I started choosing projects or spending lots of capital without their input.

Yet there are still businesses that fail to see that the relationships they have with customers and employees, especially, require this same kind of openness and engagement. Trust is built through vulnerability. The CEO or the executive team keeps its secrets and seems to patronizingly pat their customers and employees on the head. "Don't worry about anything," they say. "Just trust us."

But after decades of corporate and national betrayal, layoffs and bankruptcies, the average American doesn't blindly trust anyone anymore. In an age of social media and constant communication, we want our leaders to tell it to us straight. We expect to know not just the catchy slogan, but what's behind this product we buy.

The lifestyle brand Patagonia, which makes everything from camping gear to cashmere sweaters, understands this, and has built its reputation on transparency. The company's commitment to the environment reflects its foundation as a provider of outdoor gear that's both multi-purpose and durable. One of the company's unique core values is, *"Cause no unnecessary harm—create the best quality product with the least impact."*

It lives out this value in its foundational decisions about materials and labor. Concerned about the chemicals in the fabric of their early shirts, the company was one of the first in the country to shift to all-organic cotton. In order to avoid troubling labor problems that were plaguing other clothing manufacturers, the Patagonia leadership made a commitment not to work with any factory that they couldn't personally visit and inspect. They communicate those values to customers through "The Footprint Chronicles," a section of their website that offers full transparency about the company's supply chain and carbon footprint. Customers can explore an interactive map, watch videos, and see where each individual product that Patagonia sells is made, all the way to the down in their coats. They've run advertising campaigns that spell out the environmental impact of making some of their most popular products—135 liters of water and 20 pounds of carbon dioxide for a single jacket—and then encouraging customers not to buy what they don't need.

In an interview in *The New York Times*, Patagonia's director of environmental strategy, Jill Dumain, says that the company's transparency doesn't universally make its customers happy—they'll get complaints that they should use more recycled material, or manufacture more in the United States, for example—but also says that it has also forged loyalty among its customers. "The reaction I feel like I heard the most was, 'I trust what you tell me on the good, because you're willing to tell me about the bad.'"[46]

Compare that to the secrecy and confusion that surrounded the public awareness of "pink slime," a phrase coined by USDA scientists to describe what the manufacturer calls "lean, finely textured beef," or LFTB.

The meat product, extracted from fatty waste products once used only in dog food and cooking oil, is treated with ammonia to kill E coli contamination, and at one point was added to up to 70% of all ground beef sold in grocery stores and meat packers. LFTB had been studied and approved, with some controversy, by the USDA, which treated it as a form of ground beef and didn't require meat packagers to list it as a separate ingredient. Consumers didn't know it was in their fast food burgers and their kids' school cafeteria taco meat until a series of media reports came out, starting with the documentary *Food, Inc.* and peaking with an eleven-part ABC News special investigation in 2012, which made the whole thing seem suspicious and misleading.

The public backlash stemmed, say most observers, from the secrecy. People didn't like finding out that the food they were already eating was treated with ammonia, or that there were unlabeled fillers in their food. The unflattering "pink slime" moniker stuck. Public attitude became, "If you're not telling me about it, what are you hiding?"

The manufacturer, Beef Product, Inc., sued ABC News for defamation. "Pink slime," they said, didn't exist; their product was just as much beef as the ground meat it was mixed with. When public outcry persisted, the family-owned business and its spokespeople complained that the media was sensationalizing the story for ratings. They refused interviews and stopped letting reporters tour their facilities. But the damage was already done. BPI's revenue plummeted 80% as major purchasers like McDonalds and most grocery store chains publicly pulled pink slime from their products. At the height of the crisis, BPI laid off more than 700 workers.

We live with a "trust gap" between brands and customers, between employers and employees, and between national leaders and the people who elect them. Privacy now looks suspiciously like secrecy, and secrets can't be trusted. After being disappointed time after time, the default attitude, it seems, has become to expect the worst. And the only way to counter that is through transparency, showing that trust is deserved, that integrity is being maintained.

In the Values Economy, you must be willing to share why you make the decisions you do, and to explain your motives, not just your directives. Don't expect blind loyalty from followers; instead, encourage others to walk beside you and to share your vision for what it can be.

Conviction vs. Compliance

Do you make critical business decisions based on what is right, or what you're required to do? If an opportunity is legal, but pricks your conscience, do you take it?

The tension between compliance and conviction has always existed in American business. Human nature doesn't always overcome its selfish nature or protect its weakest members, and government exists to protect the most vulnerable of citizens. It took legal intervention to end child labor, close sweatshops, and tear down deathtrap tenement housing. It took government intervention to integrate schools and workplaces.

But every time we have to turn to rules, that compliance comes with a trust cost that has real-world consequences. And most business leaders would agree that we're turning to regulation more and more today, at the financial expense of many industries.

After the banking scandals and economic collapse of the late 2000s, Congress stepped in and, in 2010, passed the most significant changes to financial regulation since the Great Depression. The Dodd-Frank Wall Street Reform and Consumer Protection Act, named after U.S. Senator Christopher J. Dodd and U.S. Representative Barney Frank, established new government agencies to monitor the performance of companies deemed "too big to fail," regulate financial systems to prevent predatory lending to consumers, and restricted the investment and trading options for banks.

The cost has been astronomical. In its first four years, some critics estimate that Dodd-Frank regulation has cost $21.8 billion in hard costs and 60.7 million hours of additional paperwork. To put that in perspective, it would take 30,370 employees working full time to complete the additional annual paperwork.[47]

That all would have been an unnecessary expense if individuals and businesses could have acted through shared values and the conviction of doing the right thing, not the transaction that brought the biggest, fastest profit. As Mark Roellig, vice president and chief counsel of Massachusetts Mutual Life Insurance Company, told an audience at the 7th Annual Global

Ethics Summit, "You've really got to move beyond just saying, 'Yes, legally we can do this' or 'No, legally we can't do that....You've got to step back and say, 'That's the right thing to do.'"[48]

Conviction is doing what is right, regardless of whether anyone sees it. Without it, we're left to our own devices, in a place that all too often ends up hurting or taking advantage of someone else. Conviction brings long-term, sustainable, trust-driven loyalty and growth.

The real magic of relationships and trust happens when we see someone who does the right thing not because they have to, but because they know it's the right thing—and then they invite us to be a part of it.

Take what happened in February 2014, when the CEO of the drug store chain CVS, Larry Merlo, announced that his company would stop selling cigarettes and tobacco products at all of its 7700 locations. Merlo, who had started his own career as a pharmacist, struggled with the contradiction of a store that existed to provide health care for consumers, while at the same time profiting from one of the most deadly health risks. "Tobacco products have no place in a setting where health care is delivered," the company announced.[49]

It was a risky move, and not prompted by any regulation or change in the marketplace laws. Tobacco was a legal, if controversial, product, and CVS reported that product sales totaled about $2 billion a year. No other major drug store chain had accepted the American Pharmacists Association's 2010 call to stop selling tobacco. The company knew that it was going to lose money, and potentially lose customers to other stores.

But Merlo had a larger vision. In a year when the national attention was focused on how Americans receive healthcare, CVS was in a place to step into the gap. They not only cut tobacco, but also positioned themselves for the future as a health care advocate organization investing in "minute" clinics in-store, creating tobacco secession programs, and urging their customers to monitor their personal health. They even changed their name to reflect their new purpose: CVS Health.

Merlo followed his conscience, and now his employees can come to work every day knowing that this is a company that cares about its customers, that truly wants them to be healthy, and that is willing to sacrifice the easy sale in order to live by its values. Their customers have a distinguishing choice when they think about where they want to go to pick up their medicines or healthcare needs: will they go to the apathetic, generic drug store, which seems to sell anything that will make them a buck, or to the business that is willing to sacrifice itself for their good? Only one really gives the message of truly caring about those they serve.

It's tragic that more businesses and individuals today aren't living by their own convictions, and must be driven by painful compliance measures. They offer only as much as they have to, and will miss out on the relationships and goodwill that come from truly becoming a member of a community.

Advocacy vs. Apathy

Is there a cause in the world that you're willing to fight for? Is there a passion beyond the bottom line that motivates you? Do you invest time and resources in something other than extending your own pleasure and power?

Perhaps the highest form of demonstrating real concern for another in any relationship is to advocate on their behalf, and to invest in doing what is best for someone else. There's a cost to that—it might be time, financial resources, or even reputation. But the benefit is something far deeper: genuine engagement in a purpose that's bigger than the bottom line.

Value-driven brands exist not only to make a profit, but also to make the world a better place in some way. The purpose varies depending on the passions and culture of the organization; it might be to spread a message, to solve a problem, or to offer an experience. A transaction economy business may exist to sell light bulbs, but in the values economy, the light bulbs are a means to an end: developing newer, safer forms of energy, or providing light to remote or dangerous areas where it's most needed. Advocacy is proactive, driving employees to give their best and drawing customers into a common cause.

Apathy, on the other hand, ignores everything past the executive's office walls. Apathetic businesses typically have a myopic focus on the spreadsheets and the bottom line, and they make their strategic decisions based only on what will benefit them in the short term. Apathy doesn't consider the consequences, and it doesn't look at the bigger picture or the opportunities.

One of the most advocacy-driven leaders I know is David Murdock, who, among his many business holdings, is the owner and CEO of Dole Fruit. We've worked with a division of Dole for several years, and my first introduction to Murdock's passion came when I looked around their Monterrey headquarters and noticed that the vending machines carried only juice and water, and that the snacks provided for employees twice a day consisted entirely of fresh vegetables and fruits.

One of the branches of the Dole business is a group called the Dole Nutrition Institute, a research and education program established "to cultivate the seeds of knowledge and provide the public with definitive, easily accessible, scientifically-validated information on nutrition and health."[50]

The group produces, among other things, a regular electronic newsletter, cookbooks, videos, brochures, and more, all of which advocate the benefits of a plant-based diet.

A cynic may look at this and see the program as self-serving. After all, Dole is, according to its materials, the world's largest provider of fresh fruit and vegetables. *Perhaps this is merely a clever way to get people to buy more pineapples.* However, those cynics haven't met David.

Reuters has called Murdock the world's oldest CEO. Forbes lists his wealth at $3.5 billon. But at ninety-two, the self-made billionaire is still fit, active, and passionate about nutrition. After a successful career in real estate, Murdock bought Dole from a struggling Hawaiian company in the mid-1980s. At about the same time, his beloved wife, Gabriele, found out she was dying of ovarian cancer. She was just forty-three. The loss affected Murdock deeply; his mother also died from cancer in her early forties. He threw himself into research about diet and other environmental factors, eventually coming to the conclusion that the secret to longevity is what we eat.

"I used to think nothing of eating a quart of whipped cream on top of strawberries," he said in a 2013 interview with *AARP.* Rather than suffering regret for not knowing what might have helped Gabriele, he says, "I decided I would do something about it."[51]

Murdock radically changed his own diet to one that is almost entirely plant based, and he started looking for ways to encourage others to do the same. He is as passionate an evangelist as I've ever met. The Dole Nutrition Institute came out of that passion, as an advocacy program for customers and families. DNI also collaborates with another of Murdock's programs, the North Carolina Research Campus. Built on the footprint of a long-closed textile mill in a rural area south of Asheville, NCRC provides space and state-of-the-art equipment for scientists and researchers from leading universities to explore the power of plants. Dozens of academic institutions and like-minded businesses use the space, making it one of the most diverse research sites in the world.

Murdock donates $15 million annually to fund specific studies at the campus, and keeps a close eye on what other teams there are learning. He wants his company to be a vehicle to show that what you eat should give life—not limit it. "I'm interested in keeping myself alive forever, and so I want to look after other people the same way I look after myself."[52]

That concept of advocacy seems foreign in a business culture where companies, especially boardrooms, esteem themselves higher than their employees and their customers. The consequences are devastating. Employees feel completely disengaged as apathetic management fails to recognize their contributions treating them as mere economic pawns moved around the chessboard in the never-ending game of financial conquest.

Consider what happened to the accounting firm Arthur Andersen, which for decades had been the gold standard of its profession and the preferred auditor of publicly traded companies.

The firm, which grew to be one of the five largest firms in the country, built its reputation for honesty throughout the twentieth century, taking the position that an accountant's responsibility was to a company's investors and the general public, not to the executives who paid them. Over time, though, the leadership of the once-meticulous firm changed. The new guard drastically cut the auditing staff and limited the oversight of the firm's ethics watchdogs. They courted clients that would not just turn over their books, but would pay additional hefty fees for Andersen's consulting services. Instead of accountants committed to honesty and accountability, records show that the Andersen leadership intentionally promoted salespeople who could woo and win deep-pocketed clients, and who were willing to bend the rules to keep them happy.[53] The biggest of those clients, Enron, was their downfall.

When the energy company collapsed in 2001, it took the accounting firm's reputation with it. Testimony about restated earnings, financial sleights of hand, and shredded documents left Andersen's reputation in tatters, and the company never recovered. Arthur Andersen surrendered its license to practice accounting in the United States after a jury returned a felony conviction for obstructing justice.

When Arthur Andersen lost sight of its own values, and stopped being an advocate of the public trust, it was left with no driving purpose but its own bottom line. It lost its greatest asset: the trust of others.

What about you? Do you see these characteristics in your business? What about in your own life? On the next page I'm going to ask you to make a decision for yourself. Are you ready?

When customers look at your business—or friends look at your life—are you living out values that will bring you long-term success, loyalty, and trust? Are you communicating relationship, purpose, transparency, conviction, and advocacy? Or are you so afraid to stand for something that you're drowning in the sea of sameness, or getting carried away by a myopic view of the bottom line?

In the Values Economy, the key to survive—and to thrive—is to set yourself apart by engaging with the world around you. Don't be afraid to take a stand.

FIVE

IT'S UP TO YOU

Joe was afraid of dying. I was tired of jumping through the same hoops, over and over, and never seeing a difference. Something else may have brought you to this place in your career. But now that you're here, the decision is yours.

Before you can find the satisfaction and success of a values-driven work life, you need to ask, **"Am I committed to this? Am I ready to choose relationships, purpose, transparency, conviction, and advocacy?"**

As we've seen, this isn't a quick-fix answer or a smooth process. It's easy to *say* that you want something more than the bottom line, and to acknowledge that what you do forty (or sixty) hours a week should be about something more than how much money it makes. But living that out will require that you dig deep, perhaps deeper than you ever have, to understand why you do what you do, and what your employees and customers mean to you. It means making hard decisions that may be controversial and possibly alienating. It means getting vulnerable, and risking yourself for something that really matters.

What I'm describing doesn't happen on the surface. It's not a quick fix way to throw around some words, give some money to a charity, and watch your customers flow back. Hypocrisy and spin have no place in the Values Economy. You have to be able to commit.

But wait, some of you are saying. *That's fine for you to say, Mike. You founded your company. You drive its culture. But I'm a cog in a much bigger corporate wheel. I don't set the culture. I can't make big, strategic decisions like this. What can I do to change our values?*

Good question.

If you are in a position of authority or executive leadership in your organization, then you have a dual opportunity at this moment—to consider both the business as a whole as well as your role in it. If your corporate culture is toxic, if the business is stagnant, or if the employee morale is abysmal, then this is your moment to step back and take stock. Are you ready for the kind of radical change that could upend the entire way you run your business?

But even if you can't call a board meeting and mandate a new values-based agenda, you still have a choice to make about the way that *you* live, and work, and how you will influence the culture around you. You can still choose to let your values drive the way that you work and the way that you interact with others.

Leadership doesn't come from a job title or a list of direct reports. It comes from an attitude of responsibility for the things that we can control and a willingness to go first. One of my favorite examples of this comes from an oft-repeated story about Mary Barra, now the CEO of General Motors. The auto industry is notoriously resistant to change, driven by tradition and bureaucracy. Efforts to radically redefine values or change systems usually fail.

When Barra was named the vice president of human resources, one of her first tasks was to address employee complaints about the company's ten-page dress code, which tried to set standards for everyone from factory floor workers to executives. The confusing and arbitrary set of rules epitomized the problem of the century-old company where no one took responsibility for themselves and leaders were bound by illogical, external constraints.

Barra's response was quick and decisive: she sent out a memo to the staff that overrode the entire dress code and replaced it with two simple words: *Dress appropriately.*

Barra didn't change the way that GM was run—at least not that year. But she took an action within her sphere of influence that was based on her values and made changes to develop the culture that she wanted to see around her.

Your journey into values may also be a gradual one. Thriving in the Values Economy is a marathon experience, not a sprint. Change happens slowly. You've got to go into this ready to change the way you think, the way you act, the way you engage with others.

You may not change the way that your employer presents itself to the world, but you can change the way you approach your place in it. "Action springs not from thought, but from a readiness for responsibility," said theologian Dietrich Bonhoeffer.

There's a metaphor that fits here, too: the bigger the ship, the more slowly it turns. If your business doesn't already have a set of influential values in place, it will take time to establish them and to start to earn back the trust of your employees and customers. If your organization has layers of management and pages of procedures, and if you've been working for years under the looming shadow of the bottom line, then stepping back and creating a culture based on something bigger will take endurance, patience, and a willingness to sacrifice.

ARE YOU READY TO BEGIN?

That's it. That's the choice you need to make. You don't need to know what your values-driven life will look like just yet. You don't even need to know what your values are. In the following chapters, we're going to get into the meat of how to establish and lead in a values-driven company. We'll talk about how to formally identify and share organizational values in a way that draws workers together. We're going to talk about how to get started, how to handle yourself in a crisis, and how to measure your success.

But none of that will help you unless you're ready to commit to try. You can't be halfhearted or lukewarm about becoming a leader in the Values Economy.

It's okay if you're not interested. There are plenty of people who live to chase the next transaction, the next paycheck, or the next big acquisition. You can continue to work under the umbrella of the five P's. If nothing I've said here resonates, or if this kind of renewal isn't what you came looking for, or if the Values Economy doesn't appeal to you, then do me a favor. Stop reading. Close this book and give it to someone else.

Or you can try something different.

It doesn't matter what your job title is. Every person has an opportunity to consider their own values and the values that they've affiliated themselves with. Every person has the opportunity to make a difference in their sphere of influence.

Something made you curious enough to pick up this book and get this far.

Something triggered that nagging sense that something's not right and that desire to live a fuller life, where your workdays are more than just spinning in the hamster wheel.

You can keep drifting through life, without purpose, or you can make a choice to change your patterns.

What do you choose?

SIX

KNOW WHAT YOU VALUE

A young man I knew through church, Keith, asked to meet with me to discuss a career change he was considering. He'd worked in real estate for more than a decade, but was starting to burn out on the constant financial and emotional roller coaster.

When we sat down to talk, he dove right in. "Do you know how big the assisted living market is right now?"

As a matter of fact, I did have some idea. My father had lived in an assisted living community for five years before he passed away, and my mother-in-law, who suffered from Alzheimer's, had lived in a facility for seniors with dementia.

My own experience was just the tip of the iceberg. Keith explained that Southern California was a prime destination for retirees and aging Baby Boomers, so the market for senior services was growing.

"What about the competition?" I asked cautiously.

Keith was clearly still imagining the size of the pie, and not how many people already had forks in their hands. "Well, there's a lot of competition.

But every hospital has a family liaison who works with patients as they're discharged. We'll get them to refer us and add clients that way."

It sounded like there were already hundreds of companies trying to get those same hospital referrals, and although Keith had an idea that he thought would help him stand out, I felt compelled to help him see the challenges of distinguishing himself in a highly commoditized field.

I don't want to sound like I'm being critical of Keith here. He is a smart, gifted, caring, and ultimately values-driven guy who was in the early stages of developing an idea. He was following the practical steps—creating a business plan, doing a competitive overview—that we've been taught are important to starting a new business. Plenty of leaders have launched a startup for worse reasons and with less planning. But as his friend and mentor, I knew that if Keith was going to succeed, he needed to be more intentional about discovering the values that would distinguish and drive him.

"I'll make you a deal," I told him. "I want you to spend a week visiting existing assisted living facilities. I'll introduce you to the staff at the place where my father lived. Talk to as many residents as you can. Ask them about their lives. Then we'll talk again."

A few weeks later, I sat down again with Keith and his business partner, Marcus. I could tell something had changed since our last encounter. Before I could ask a question, Keith started to tell me, in great detail, about several of the people he'd met. He knew their names. He knew their stories. He understood how hard it was for them to give up their independence, and how important it was for them to hold on to their stories.

"When I thought about assisted living services I was thinking about the revenue potential. But now…" He started to tell me about his grandmother,

Eleanore. Keith described her as a natural caretaker. She was the oldest of six children, a Navy Hospital Corpsman in World War II, and the mother of twelve. She'd raised her family in a neighborhood full of large Irish families, and she'd been the advisor, comforter, and informal nurse for many of them. "She was always patching together someone's kid," Keith told me, "and her kitchen was full of women, all the time."

Eleanore developed Alzheimer's at the end of her life, and spent the final months of her life in a nursing home ward. Even there, she reached out and made friends.

"She took care of people her whole life." Keith looked at me, and his eyes were shining. "And now we can do something in her name. I want to do senior care, Mike, and I want to call it Eleanore's Friends, in her honor."

"What makes that different?" I pushed.

"The legacy. People are scared of losing their parents. Seniors are afraid their legacy will disappear. I want to protect that. I want to honor the people who come to us, like my grandmother honored people. I want to help them live in their homes as long as possible. I want to hire a staff and get volunteers who love people, who will pour into these families."

He'd started to discover his purpose. Over the next few months we went through a process to articulate his new company's values and discover ways to connect those to his audience. When Eleanore's Friends launched, it was under the values umbrella of celebrating lives. I love the words they use on their website:

We respect and honor people as unique individuals with feelings like our own. Their lives have dignity and value that must be reinforced and guarded during their most vulnerable years. We're committed to providing a wide

100

range of care, yet offering it as a loving family member or friend would, because homecare is a very personal act of service.

Keith exudes values of compassion, connection, and companionship. He invests some of his profits back into a foundation that pays for home care for seniors who can't afford it. And he does it all with a level of integrity that would make his grandmother proud.

WHAT DO YOU VALUE?

The hunt for values is a deeply personal journey. Yet the process of formally identifying, articulating, and reviewing values is also a valuable opportunity for businesses of every size and age.

If you're one of those people I described in the Introduction, who are struggling to know if "this is all there is," chances are that you or your company have lost track—or never found—your own values. This chapter is for you.

When we don't intentionally stop and choose what values will drive us, both as individuals and as businesses, we leave our core identity in the hands of others—friends, competitors, media, or our own mistaken notion of public opinion. I've met too many people, and consulted with too many companies, that have forced themselves into awkward, unnatural molds of what they thought they should be in order to "fit in" or "compete." They try to be aggressive when their nature is to be cooperative, or they cut corners to fit someone else's timeline of expectations. They end up leading fractured lives, never being really honest with themselves or the people around them, and they miss out on what matters most. These are the leaders most vulnerable to the temptations of the transaction, or to taking an unethical shortcut.

For brands, this uncertainty results in what we would classify as an identity crisis. Many of the companies I've engaged with over the years suffer a lack of vision that springs from muddy values. Middle managers wander aimlessly through their days, moving from meeting to meeting without any sense as to how what they're doing fits the overall direction of the company. Workers go through the motions without any emotional investment in the outcome. The feeling of lethargy, or even despair, is palpable.

Even if you think your business has articulated a mission or list of principles, take this opportunity to go back and evaluate whether they hold true today. Going through the process may show you what's already there. If there's some barrier to enacting them or living them out, you'll find that, as well. And if you discover you don't like your values, then this is the first step to changing them.

The following steps are an outline of the comprehensive process that The Values Institute takes with our clients to formally establish or redefine a business' values. If you are in a senior position of authority within your organization, you can use these as a guide to begin your own internal process with your customers and staff. If your job title doesn't allow you to oversee the redevelopment of your entire organization, don't despair. These same steps can help you define the values of a department, a project, or even just what happens inside your own cubicle.

STEP 1: IDENTIFY YOUR PERSONAL VALUES

Before you cast your net over your entire business, be sure you know what you value as an individual, and what drives you.

My own journey began when I remembered a quote: "The most important thing in life is finding the most important thing." That sent me on a months-long journey to articulate what I stood for, and what I wanted to stand for. I talked to my wife and to friends and coworkers who knew me well. I paid attention to how I made decisions and looked at the things that made me unique from the people around me.

Your process might be similar. What do you value most? What are the purposes and priorities that make you a unique, fulfilled human being? It might be your integrity, which drives you to honesty above all. It might be your sensitivity and skill as an encourager. You may value stability, or independence, or justice. It may be your loyalty, or your faith, or your family.

If you're not sure what your personal values are, spend a week paying attention to where you put your energy or emotional attention in an average day. What do you spend most of your time thinking about? What influences your decisions in difficult situations? How do you approach conflict? As Ralph Waldo Emerson said, "That which dominates our imagination and our thoughts will determine our lives and our character."

Another good way to identify your values is to seek the input of the people who know you best. Many times, the friends, colleagues, and family members who see you every day will be able to articulate what is so close to you that you can't see it. That's what happened for my wife, Dana, a few years ago when she established a foundation to help women left unexpectedly single after a death or divorce. Dana struggled to know how to define her fledgling program from the dozens of public and private support services already in place. But for me, and for her closest group of supporters and friends, the answers were obvious. Dana's Upper Room foundation (named after Jesus washing the disciple's feet and the reflected the values that defined Dana herself: *humility* (the grants are made anonymously), *commitment* (supporting women long past the "crisis" window when most support disappears), *empowerment* (enabling women to help one another and give back), *faith*, and *authenticity*.

This kind of clear-eyed assessment requires vulnerability. For some people, this is a difficult process and reveals some things about the ways that they're living that they don't like. If your initial impression of what drives you doesn't match up with the reality of how you invest your time and make your decisions, take a step back to consider which side is in conflict: are you not living out your values, or do you really value something other than what you originally thought? Work through these conflicts until you have the list of values that *should* guide your decisions.

STEP 2: IDENTIFY YOUR BUSINESS VALUES

Once you've gotten comfortable with the process of evaluating your personal values, take what you've learned and look at your business in the same way. This is usually a more difficult process, especially for bigger, or older, businesses, where there are more stakeholders bringing their own experiences and personal visions to the same table. But every brand has a story of values if they take the time to uncover it.

What is the purpose of your business? Is it growing the stock price? The development of disruptive ideas? The creation of community? Steady growth to new customers, or explosive growth to new areas? Does the company value its employees? Remember, that's not just something that the CEO tells the press. Look at where the organization puts its time, energy, and non-fixed financial resources. What drives management's decisions in difficult or controversial decisions?

If you're not sure where to start, look at the company's history. At some point in your history, your business was founded on values. See what is already embedded in your organizational DNA. If you aren't the original founder, interview your veteran leaders and employees to uncover the origin story of the company. Somewhere in there you'll find a series of guiding principles and priorities that drove your business into existence. They may have never migrated from the dreams of a CEO to the rest of the company, or they may have gotten lost in a series of mergers and in rapid growth (or slow decline). Values get lost over time, or shift due to a change of leadership.

Those existing values and "rules of engagement" are worth digging for and revisiting. It's far easier, and more natural, to reinvest in an existing story and purpose than it is to try to launch and manage an entirely new set of goals. I don't say that to discourage you from "stretch goals" and visionary thinking. In fact, if your organization has undergone major changes over time, or if you discover that your business' original goals might be a barrier to growth, a new vision and set of values will give you a new horizon line and a chance to set a new course.

Then, do something riskier: ask the people around you what they think the business values, and see how they match up.

These values, if adopted, won't change without major, monumental shifts, just as your personal values are deeply engrained in you and don't change just because you get a promotion or move to a new house. So it's important to engage both senior management and a cross-functional group of influential employees and stakeholders, regardless of title. Depending on your business, you may even choose to solicit the perspective of selected customers. Ask specific questions to draw out different perspectives. For example:

What is the purpose of this business/organization/department?

What makes us unique?

Why do you work here?

What is the legacy you want to leave?

What would our customers say about our relationships with them?

What are the best-kept secrets of this company?

Who are our real competitors?

Choosing a business' values and committing an entire organization to them isn't something to take on lightly, and it's certainly not something to do alone. You can't define the values of an entire organization from within a vacuum.

Too often, corporate values are decided in the same way that the Catholic Church decides the Pope—a handful of leaders sequesters themselves for a series of secret conversations and no transparency. They emerge with a puff of smoke and a list of new words and values, and nobody knows how the decisions were made—even the wide-reaching, philosophically challenging ones. They say only, "Trust us, we know what's best."

Of course, human beings don't want to be told what to trust. As we've seen, that's not how the process works. And so employees rebel, and they represent the brand without any loyalty or connection to what it stands for. If they haven't been invited to contribute or ascribe to the values, they won't.

That's a lesson I learned not long ago, when a local hospital hired us to help promote a new program. We started the project the way we always do: "Let's look at your values." The executive in charge of the campaign gave us a list of words that looked admirable, but I noticed that they were the same compliant values that every other healthcare company in the country was using. At the top of the list was *excellence*.

106

"Okay," I said. "Let's talk about what this means. What does *excellence* mean to the charge nurse who's working the eleventh hour of her twelve-hour shift?"

You see most organizations we meet have never taken the discussion of values to their front-line staff—not because they don't care, but because they've never seen it done before.

So that's where we started—not with an ad campaign or a new logo, but with a series of conversations with key hospital stakeholders. We talked to charge nurses, to the families of patients, to office workers, to doctors, and to community advocates and volunteers. We asked all of them what drove them to do their jobs, and what this particular hospital stood for. What we heard largely aligned with what the executives had identified. The staff did, indeed, value excellence. But there was another word that kept coming up that seemed to come completely out of left field.

Ferocity.

The hospital staff were passionate people who didn't just come to work; they *attacked* their jobs. They saw their calling as *ferocious*: The ferocious determination of a doctor to find a treatment that works. The ferocious love that a parent feels for her child as she relinquishes control to the nurses in the oncology ward. The ferocious commitment of the physical therapy staff to help an accident victim walk again, and of a donor to support the quest to find a cure.

Ferocity was the word that could motivate a charge nurse in her eleventh hour. It was a term that could inspire the development staff to be brave in seeking new funding. It could inspire confidence in the customers—the patients and the families of patients—who were asked to trust the hospital in

107

the most vulnerable moments of their lives. It was a word that could start a lot of conversations, and would help to align this staff and community. But that idea didn't come from the top of the organization. It came from the people who were living the values every day, and just needed to be invited to put words to it.

After all, as we've seen, values aren't what we define for ourselves; they're what we live out. You can say you value thrift, but if you're driving around in a fancy sports car and wearing designer clothes, that's not the value that you're sharing. Your company can say it values its heritage, but if you're closing factories and outsourcing to a company with lax child labor laws, you've got a problem.

STEP 3: KNOW WHO YOU'RE WORKING FOR

Once you have input from your stakeholders, and feel like you have a clear sense of what makes your company different (or what can make your company different), and what passions drive your business, be intentional about running it through the filters we established in Chapter 4:

Does this value exist to benefit others, or to hurt others?

Does this value build trust?

If you can't put faces to the stakeholders of your values, and you can't clearly show how your ideas are benefitting someone specific, then you may still be working with compliant ideas, or with a list of values based on the self-focused Five Ps. But if you can show that these values not only define you but also prepare you to build relationships of trust, you're on to something.

There is perhaps no company in contemporary business that's as famous—or as infamous, depending on your perspective—for its laser-focused values as Amazon. Ever since 1995, when it first packaged and shipped a book called *Fluid Concepts and Creative Analogies* to a computer scientist in Los Gatos, California, Jeff Bezos and the Amazon.com team have been committed to providing the best possible experience for the customer. Creating an intuitive, comprehensive user experience is their core value, and the very first line of their Leadership Principles touts their primary value: *Customer Obsession*:

Leaders start with the customer and work backwards. They work vigorously to earn and keep customer trust. Although leaders pay attention to competitors, they obsess over customers.[54]

"We see our customers as invited guests to a party, and we are the hosts. It's our job every day to make every important aspect of the customer experience a little bit better," says Bezos.[55] His customers love the service; year after year the American Customer Satisfaction Index ranks Amazon with the highest customer satisfaction across all brands.[56]

Yet living out values like this, with such a total focus on one set of stakeholders, doesn't make the company universally popular. Obsession can be a divisive word, and Amazon is one of the most controversial American companies so far in the twenty-first century. Does their commitment to customers come at too high a cost? Its vendors, from book publishers to toy makers, complain that Amazon's rapidly growing market share empowers it to make unfair demands, affecting the suppliers' ability to stay in business. The workplace environment for both office and warehouse jobs is reportedly sometimes intense, even antagonistic.

Other businesses, led by other teams, approach their values and identify their audiences differently. Patagonia sees its manufacturers and supply chain as the critical part of what sets them apart. TOMS Shoes is working not just for their paying customers, but for children who need shoes. That's what makes each organization unique and protects us from the sea of sameness. What matters is that you are intentional about identifying who matters to you.

What are you doing for them?

How do these values build relationships and common bonds with them?

If your company disappeared tomorrow, would your customers care? Could they seamlessly shift to a competitor? Or does your company stand for something so powerful in the marketplace that it simply couldn't be replaced?

STEP 4: COMMIT YOUR VALUES TO PAPER

In this day of Instagrammed photos and live streaming, it's easy to lose sight of the value of writing things down. But as you filter through the ideas and values that come from the discovery process, take the time, as a group, to write them down. Creating a list of words and ideas that represent the core values of your unique business creates a sense of weight and importance. It's harder to ignore something once it's formalized.

Writing down your emerging list of values says "we were here, and this is why." It's like the earliest paintings found in caves. It's a chance to make your mark in a way that others can see—and hold you accountable.

As I've said before, there is no list of "good" values to choose from. What you develop will be a reflection of who you are—it could be single words or full sentences. Be as descriptive as you need to be. Don't base these ideas on anything that your competitors are doing or what you think your customers want to hear. Focus on your business' story, and what influences and inspires you.

STEP 5: DEFINE YOUR VALUES

Knowing that *ferocity* is what sets your hospital apart or that your amusement park is there to provide *magical moments* is great. But in order to bring your whole team or staff around to an idea, you need to be clear and consistent with what it means.

Once your organization has identified your list of core values, the next step is to first define them, and then prioritize. Without taking this formal step, you risk trying to manage a list of too many words and not enough substance.

For each word that your group has identified, take the time to agree on a definition that offers a clear understanding of the intent and spirit of a particular value. Words can be tricky. Most values, when taken without a clarifying definition, can be interpreted in a variety of ways and can leave your employees and stakeholders without the clear vision that you need them to have.

One of the values that defines our agency is *imagination*. It's a great word, full of whimsy, but how does it play out in a company? What does imagination look like in the accounting department or for the heroes who keep our IT working? We defined *imagination* this way: creative curiosity that challenges us to pursue the idea that anything is possible.

Anything is possible. Those three words have changed our culture. They've freed our staff—not just those in the traditionally creative departments, but everyone—to see this as a place where they can explore the unconventional ideas and think optimistically.

Once you understand what you mean by the list of core values, make sure that each one is truly an influential value and not merely a compliant placeholder. If a value has slipped onto the list but is difficult to measure, doesn't serve a key stakeholder, or lacks an organization-specific application, take it off. Focus on what makes your company unique, and what will inspire your customers to give you their trust.

At the end of the process, you should hopefully have trimmed your list to a manageable number of values. We find that most organizations can focus on no more than eight at a time.

According to our research, what's most important isn't the word that an organization chooses to describe their value, but the way that they express it to their community of employees and customers.

By the time my friend Keith and his business partner launched Eleanore's Friends, they had developed a clear, measureable, and influential list of values that would drive the organization for years to come, and that would set them apart from their competitors:

Empathy: We identify with the feelings, thoughts, and concerns of those who come to us for care and vow to preserve their dignity because of our shared personal experiences.

Legacy: We desire to leave behind a lasting reminder, something of extreme value handed down from the past, which will outlast generations.

Servanthood: We believe that in service of another, we find out true purpose.

Hope: We hold true to an eternal, optimistic viewpoint that all will turn out according to plan, and we share that belief with all we serve.

Family: We care for families, the cornerstone of a healthy society and the focus of our practice, bound together by one commitment and treated with utmost respect.

Comfort: We strive to soothe, console, talk, listen, laugh, cry, and reassure in times of greatest need.

Integrity: We adhere to moral and ethical principles. We say what we mean, mean what we say, and act accordingly. We resolve to do what we know is right in every circumstance.

STEP 6: COMMUNICATE YOUR VALUES

If your values never make it out of the boardroom, they'll never influence the way you do business. Hopefully, if this is an organization-wide process, everyone from the receptionist to the chairman of the board has contributed their experiences and opinion in some way already, and has invested their own perspective to the process. The values of an organization belong to everyone.

But at some point you've had to filter all of that input, and prioritize it into an actionable, influential overview of major principles. What they need at this point is to see how their feedback has been molded into a formal statement, the commitment of the leadership to the values, and the way to understand exactly what these values mean when they're lived out in the everyday. What are the expectations for the staff, the team, and the leadership going forward?

Develop a plan for rolling out the new (or newly articulated) values to a staff, and make it an event they'll remember. This is a sea change moment for your business, and it deserves something more than new posters and an article in the company newsletter.

How will these values change the way you do business?

It's important here to be prepared for some pushback. If you have developed truly influential values and ideas that plant a flag and stand for something, it's likely that not everyone will agree with the new direction. If a handful of employees, or even senior leaders, are resistant to the values that the organization has established, then they're essentially saying that they can't support the very core of what your business is about. A single executive in a position of authority can have a powerful effect on how a company communicates its story and purpose. It's better to let an employee go than to let them poison the organization from within.

If the overall response to your rollout is lukewarm, though, and you don't sense buy-in across the organization, then the process itself may have overlooked some key insight into the core of the business. Do these values truly represent the feelings, passions, and feedback of the group, or are they a reflection of your own preferences and personal values? Did you miss something in the previous steps?

YOU'RE NOT DONE YET

Values, even once they're written down and shared, don't truly become influential until they're lived out. Once you've formally identified and owned a purpose that will set you apart, the final step is to live it out—a concept so important that we'll spend the entire next chapter talking about it.

The people who work near you and for you must see clearly how you make values part of your work and your life, from a new product or partnership to a staffing decision. You see, true transformation happens only if your own behavior supports your values. What should they expect from you? If you value transparency, start by being open with your employees and customers. If you value leadership, then be present, purposeful, and clear.

Without identifying behaviors that support your values, those very values are in danger of becoming nothing more than empty promises, so it's imperative that for each defined value a corresponding behavior be established to add necessary clarity, consistency and accountability.

A few months after Keith launched Eleanore's Friends, he was still struggling for a way to break into the market. After a series of disappointing dead ends, he finally got to make his pitch to the executive of an influential health care company. The talk went well, and the man offered to send referrals to Eleanore's Friends. Keith was elated; this was just the open door he needed. But the exec kept talking. He had a list of the preferred "perks" that his staff liked to receive from their vendors.

Keith froze. What would Eleanore say? With a pounding heart, he thanked the executive for his support, and in the same breath let him know that there would be no "perks." Eleanore's Friends would need to grow based on its values and its service, not what it bought. The man seemed shocked; it appeared that no one had ever turned him down before. The meeting ended shortly after.

Keith trudged back to the parking lot. He'd done the right thing, but business success still seemed just beyond his grasp.

As he got into his car, his phone rang. An administrator from a different hospital was calling out of the blue. She'd seen one of his pamphlets. "We already have a system for referring patients to services when they're discharged," she told him. "But this thing you're describing really speaks to me. I have to meet you." They did, and Keith told her about Eleanore. Today that hospital is one of his biggest referrers.

I've never seen an example of values that paid off so immediately.

SEVEN

SHARING YOUR VAUES

The process of defining your values is a critical first step. But what really affects the future of an organization, and the satisfaction of the people who run it, is what you do with those values once you've introduced them. Time and time again I've seen values squandered because they never made it out of the boardroom. Employees are left to wade through the mundane details of the everyday, and customers see only the bottom line. But I've also seen inspiring examples of how a company's unique identity and values, when they infuse every decision, can make a difference in even the least likely operations.

Not long ago, The Values Institute started working with a new client, a company that runs a network of for-profit colleges and adult education programs across the country. Their industry had recently taken a series of public hits as several of their competitors were punished for not delivering enough value to vulnerable students. While our new client had never had a problem with standards or compliance, their CEO acknowledged that public opinion was generally against them. He came to us and said, "We have a company, but now we need a brand." He wanted to do something to help him communicate what made his company unique, and trustworthy, in their field.

In our parlance, he needed to articulate and share his company's unique values.

The Institute's first step was, as always, to interview the most important stakeholders in a company's values: the employees and the customers. I'll admit that I went into those first conversations expecting to find a demoralized staff. Their industry had been taking a beating from the media for months, and I expected that would take a toll. But to my surprise, I met some of the most dedicated, caring, tenacious employees I'd ever interviewed. Almost to a person, these were individuals who loved their jobs and understood what they were working for.

One senior executive we talked to admitted that she sometimes had to defend her job to friends and family. "People don't understand how much we care about these students," she said. "Some of the adults I work with have never had anyone show faith in them. We believe in them. Being here gives me the chance to see people blossom." Another described the influence of her supervisor, who would drive to a student's house and bring them to class if they were having transportation issues, and who encouraged her to take the time to understand each student's individual situation and potential.

When we talked to the students, we heard similar stories of tenacious commitment. The cost of the program rarely came up. Instead, the "customers" of the school wanted to talk about their teachers, and their own journeys of self discovery, and how they were discovering hope for their own futures. They talked about the inspiration of working with teachers who had once been students in the same programs, and the ways that those teachers modeled success and potential. The tenacious commitment and loyalty of their instructors was contagious, and the relational values of the programs were rubbing off.

In the midst of external crises and public pressure that could crush the spirit of a less grounded organization, this particular company stands out and shines. They're not playing defense, investing themselves in compliance or accreditation issues. Instead, this was a company that understood what they were there to do. Their customers are loyal and their employees are focused *because they know why they're here.*

To really engage with the Values Economy, it's not enough to make a list of what matters. You need to consistently and accurately share and model that purpose. Your values are your true business currency, arguably more important than even your products. So shout them from the rooftops. Use your company newsletters, corporate events, staff and team meetings, and even performance reviews to reinforce the story of your brand internally. Externally, use your values as your most powerful communications asset in your marketing, in your product choices, and in the ways that every employee interacts with your customers. As author Simon Sinek says, "People don't buy what you do, they buy why you do it."

Not only will you attract the kind of customers that will fuel your business, you will reinforce in the minds and hearts of your employees why they made the right choice in working for and remaining loyal to your company.

DO YOUR EMPLOYEES KNOW WHY THEY'RE HERE?

Gary Kelly, CEO of Southwest Airlines, famously said, "Our people are our single greatest strength and most enduring long-term competitive advantage."

And he's right. A corporation, remember, is a fancy word for a group of people with a shared purpose. And when it comes to what makes a company stand out in the sea of sameness, it all comes down to how the values are lived out day by day, person by person.

That's why your job as a leader in the Values Economy isn't done once you identify and roll out your new set of core values. Are your values the center of your communications with your employees and direct reports? I don't just mean those specific quarterly meetings when you take the executive team on an off-site retreat, or your intentional effort to greet everyone at the company holiday party. I mean really getting out there, to the place where your business happens every day, and showing the people who are your front line of service why they're important, and what they're bringing.

Every cook in a food service business should know how their job relates to the company's values. *I'm not just giving this person a hamburger. I'm giving them a moment of happiness.* Every shift manager should understand how her job fits into a lasting vision. *I'm not here to create a schedule and make sure everyone shows up on time; I'm here to build a community that provides something our customers need.*

But communicating values goes deeper than the front line. In some cases, it's easy to show the people who work with your customers every day how the values affect them. But what about the people in between—those brave souls who spend their days with inventories and spreadsheets? Their choices deeply affect a company's values, too.

In a values-driven organization, every senior and middle manager should buy in and be ready to represent your shared values.

In many larger businesses, this is harder than inspiring the front lines.

119

Middle managers often don't have an opportunity to see, firsthand, the impact of their attitude on customers and products. Their jobs leave them distracted by routine, not face-to-face with customers. It's easier to get caught up in supervising or spreadsheets and forget why they're there in the first place. Yet they are the people empowered with the opportunity and responsibility to evangelize a brand's values on a daily basis, and to guide the people who work for them. If they're not on board, then their teams will be caught in the crossfire of conflict and hypocrisy.

I've also seen leaders, like the college's CEO I mentioned earlier in the chapter, who have stepped up to take their headquarters perspective to the field. These leaders hire people who share and demonstrate their values, and then listen—*really listen*—to the feedback they get. The result is a motivated, dedicated workforce. In a values-driven company, a manager knows that their job is not functional—to oversee sales, or create operational efficiencies, or design marketing messaging, etc. A true loyalist knows that their job is to be the banner carrier and evangelist of their company's values.

That all sounds good, but it's not easy to consistently communicate values to a diverse, often geographically scattered, workforce. What will motivate your organization, and your employees, to buy in to a new paradigm?

The answer will look different for each company, based on your size, your demographics, and how much trust you've already established—or lost—with your workforce. But no matter who you are or how big your company is, I can tell you what *won't* work: money. Engagement doesn't happen because a job has a certain salary, or because your product is the least expensive. It happens when you can connect with others and show them that your brand is about more than money.

In the Transaction Economy, employee loyalty seemed like something you could buy. Salaries kept rising. Stock options soared. Pension plans promised a lifetime of security. In an economy where the quality of life kept improving, employees seemed content, and business kept growing. But money built only a shallow trust, and when it started to disappear, so did the loyalty.

Study after study show that our paychecks aren't what motivate us to be our best selves at work. Money gets us into the building to punch a clock. But in most studies workers say they would trade a higher salary for less tangible, more values-based rewards like appreciation and a sense of camaraderie with a team. This is particularly true of Millennials, who are pointed about choosing to work for companies that have a clearly defined purpose and contribute to society in greater ways, rather than companies with strong profits and a focus on financial gain.

This is the future of our workplaces and our successful brands. We need something more. We need what researcher Josh Bersin calls the Irresistible Organization, "where workers feel passionate about their company's mission and feel supported by an inspiring, humanistic work environment."[57] That sounds to me a lot like another way of saying shared values.

In the new economy, we've seen that companies collapse. Pension plans crumble. Income has become a wedge between senior leaders and front-line workers. We've learned to look for meaning beyond the stability of a paycheck. We've learned to look for shared values.

I was reminded of this principle not long ago, when my own son started a new job. Zach is now twenty-seven, and has been pursuing entrepreneurial projects and startups for his whole adult life. After a few years of roller coaster income, he got married and decided to try something that came with benefits and a more stable income. He's working as a liaison between a hospital and the healthcare company he works for, which is a perfect fit for his education in health science and his background in sales.

After the first week of training, we had dinner, and my son's eyes were just shining. He didn't want to talk about his salary or his benefits package. He wanted to tell me about his day. One of Zach's jobs is to meet with patients and show them how to use the equipment that his company provides. His first client had been a woman who was being discharged, and it was his job to teach her how to use the oxygen machine that she would need to be comfortable. "It's pretty cool to be part of something that's doing really good stuff for people," he said. And then, almost as an afterthought, "And I'm getting paid for it."

His employer taught him how to sell a product. He discoverd the opportunity to experience *why* he was selling a product.

WHAT DO YOUR CUSTOMERS SEE?

Your values impact not only your employees, but also the people who support you and allow your business to continue: your customers. And by customers, I don't just mean the person who hands over their credit card at the register and buys something. Depending on your business type, your customers are the ones who use your services and keep you in business. That might mean the person who buys your product, but it's also your donors, your subscribers, your users, your clients, your members, the parents of your members, and more.

In advertising, we spend a lot of time identifying the demographic of a brand's customer. But there's more to a person than *single male, making more* *than $75,000 a year, renting.* In the crush associated with getting the next sale, brands seem to have forgotten that there's a person on the other side of that sale, or that phone call, or that email. Beyond the fact that our latest product offering will rock their world, what do we know about them? What do they need? What do they desire? And how could you help them get there? That's where your values overlap, and where a shared connection will build trust.

Take the time to study your customer. Get out of the office. Get out from behind the counter. Have a conversation that goes beyond "what can I sell you?"

Umair Haque, director of the research center Havas Media Labs, described in an interview with *Fast Company* how brands can create real value: "Did this brand make you fitter, wiser, smarter, closer? Did it improve your personal outcomes? Did it improve your community outcomes? Did it pollute the environment? We're trying to get beyond did this company make a slightly better product to the more resonant, meaningful question: Did this brand actually impact your life in a tangible, lasting, and positive way?"[58]

Your customers are people, not just consumers. To drive this message and priority home, try to ban the word consumer from your office. Calling them consumers devalues them. It dehumanizes them. Your customers are people, with kids and aging parents to care for, and student loans to pay, and a car that needs an oil change. They stay awake at night thinking about the future. They're more than what they buy.

If your purpose is to create and distribute an innovative new game that will engage imaginations and stretch the capabilities of technology, how does that measure up to what your customer needs and wants? Are they testing their skills? Are they looking for immersive entertainment? Will you meet them in the place of non-stop thrills or in a deeply immersive story? How does that reflect your values?

Every customer should be able to see, at least intuitively, what sets you apart and why they're choosing to engage with you and not your competitor. *I'm buying this car because this company values safety and has thought about what my family needs. I'm signing up for membership with this website because they are passionate about this area that I'm passionate about.*

If you surveyed your customers, would they be able to identify what you stand for? Would they know not just what you do, but what your purpose is in doing it? There's more to customer communication than putting a page three levels down on your website that lists your company values. Be honest: most people aren't reading that.

What can you give them that will show them that you understand?

In January 2015, the government-funded organization Sport England noticed that one-third of all women in the UK didn't exercise. They wanted to change that, but the challenge was how to do something different. There were plenty of ads and articles and celebrity spokespeople who all told women that they should be more active. What would it take to change that?

In an interview with *The Huffington Post*, Sport England Executive Director Tanya Joseph said, "We did lots of research, and there was one single unifying theme—fear of judgment."[59] Women were self conscious of their bodies, worried about taking time away from their families, and generally uncomfortable with what they would look like. So the group found real women of all ages and body shapes, and created a YouTube video that showed them doing the things they love: swimming, dancing, boxing, playing soccer, and more. None of them look like Olympic athletes, but they're all incredibly happy and satisfied. "I'm slow, but I'm lapping everyone on the couch" are the words imposed over a smiling, middle aged woman on a bicycle. It was an empowering message that immediately wet viral, garnering more than 7 million views in the first month.

Why? Shared values. Sport England took a body-positive message that empathized with what the audience really wanted, and inspired them to get there. They established themselves as a partner in the quest for good health.

Sport England succeeded because they listened before they spoke, and then they gave their customer a message that could be embraced.

Too many businesses today jump into trying to talk to their customers before they have anything to say. "We should be on social media," say the serious executives who have never looked at a Twitter feed, let alone created one. "Customers love social media."

I don't dispute that. Public trust in a company measurably improves when their CEO is personally active on the democratic social media platform of Twitter, where every user has an equally limited number of characters to publicly share their thoughts with anyone who wants to listen.[60] But here's the catch: before you can talk to your customers, you need to have something to say. If your only interest is in selling them your new release or advertising a sale, your brand will fail the "social" test. You'll be shouting about transactions in a place where everyone else is talking about what really matters.

Your values give you a place to talk to your customers about something other than your profit margin. If you know that you both value creativity, use the social spaces to highlight and celebrate other expressions of creativity. Honor the work of others. Jacqueline Summers, CEO of Ann Summers, uses her personal Twitter feed not only to promote her company's clothing line, but also to sponsor a weekly contest to support other female entrepreneurs. Google famously uses its home page not only to drive people to its search, but to promote curiosity with a new, illustration that changes daily. Those kinds of behaviors are values-driven, not sales driven.

Customer loyalty is built by something much bigger than stamps or hole punches on a frayed card in my wallet. Sure, a rewards card might get a customer to come back through the door, but it doesn't build the positive responses that will make them an evangelist and truly loyal, trusting member of your community. It won't drive them to the kind of word-of-mouth messages that are worth twice what a brand will get from paid advertising.

Incentives aren't the same as loyalty. The true, customer-based relationship is nurtured after the transaction occurs. It happens through the conversation the customer has with your employees after the loyalty card is punched, and the level of comfort they find in your store. It's about constantly building trust through shared beliefs, desires, and—yes—values.

YOUR JOB IS THE BACKDROP

Relationships based on shared values can't be bought and they can't be mandated; they must be engaged and inspired into being. And the best way to engage and inspire is to lead by example.

I've told you that there was a time, right after the culture-changing events of 9-11 and before we started to research this idea of values, when I was feeling tired in my career and uncertain of my purpose. We'd been fired by a major client in a way that left me smarting. What was the point of all my hard work? One night during that difficult season, I was complaining to my wife, as I was wont to do.

And, as she was wont to do, she didn't offer me undeserved sympathy. "Stop whining," she reminded me, none too gently. "Do you really think God put you here to demonstrate your advertising prowess? Advertising is what you do; it's not who you are. You have a bigger mission—to build relationships. Those clients are just the backdrop for relationships to happen."

Those were powerful words, and a good reminder of my true values. A client had once called our advertising agency the "West Coast agency with a Midwest conscience." I took it as a compliment. We may have changed the name on the website banner a few times over the years, but the values were the same: to be genuine, service-oriented, and committed to advocating on behalf of the people and issues we care about. We held our relationships with clients as a sign of trust. In an industry where agencies can form, sign clients, make a million dollars, lose clients, and go out of business in a single year, our staff dug in. We attended clients' weddings, then baby showers, then bar mitzvahs. We deeply ingrained ourselves in the personal side of our business relationships because we inherently believed that we would prosper by being good to our people and being good to our customers.

My wife reminded me of that, and it became an important part of the message that The Values Institute shares with clients: **The first step of being a leader in a values-driven company is to live those values out in your personal life.**

If my agency was going to plant our agency's flag and our reputation on this idea of trust, then that was my purpose, too.

My job wasn't to go to work and close my door, get things done, and go home. I wasn't in advertising so that I could spend all of my time in meetings, wooing new clients and building the bottom line. As a founder and leader, I was the keeper of what we later defined as our own company values: imagination, character, fearlessness, diversity, belief and joy. That didn't change just because a brand wanted to skip off to what looked like richer pastures.

You probably spend more time at work than you do with your family. If your workplace doesn't express our values, then you're left living a half-baked life, stretched thin between priorities that never quite connect.

Check your values against what you do every day: do you filter your new business opportunities through your values? When you hire a new employee, are you intentionally looking for someone who shares your company's values, or are you simply looking for the first person who can fill the hole in the org chart? Do you reward your direct reports strictly for functional performance, or do you also look for ways to acknowledge the ways they support the culture around them? People are watching.

If my business says that it values respect for others, then I must keep my temper and not treat the people who work with me as if they are inferior. If we value environmental responsibility, then the car I drive and the clothes I wear should reflect that. If we value creativity, then I must allow out-of-the-box thinking, even when it contradicts my own ideas. If we value quality, then the decisions I make about everything from staffing to vendors must reflect the idea that cheapest is not best.

*

WHAT LEADERSHIP LOOKS LIKE

It all comes down to leadership. If the influential voices at the top of an organization live out their company's values, the people around them will be drawn to follow. If they live as hypocrites, the structure will collapse.

Employees who are left feeling ignored or customers who feel unappreciated may consider other, more appealing options.

But what does that look like in practice?

We've identified three critical ways that a leader can demonstrate their company's values and unify their staff around a mission.

Leaders listen. When leaders are driven by fear and greed, they become blind to the needs of others. They start looking out only for themselves and their own bottom lines. But leaders who are driven by values bigger than their own self interest seek input on better processes, new ideas, and customer feedback. They listen as much—or more—than they talk. They respect each member of their team—including their customers—as someone who is a critical part of their purpose.

It's easy to get caught up in the responsibilities and routines of the headquarters office and lose track of the front line. But if a company's shared values aren't reaching the customer, there's something missing.

At our agency, my partners and I try to live this out by being intentional about who we invite to join our staff. Finding those who will fit into our unique culture is important. The wrong person can throw off the entire energy of a small business like ours. The right person can fill us with enthusiasm and bring a fresh perspective to how we understand our daily experience.

When we interview potential candidates, we don't spend a lot of time discussing their past experience or asking what kind of degree they have. Instead, we ask open-ended questions about how they perceive themselves and how they would handle certain situations, and then we listen to how they handle the questions. We're looking for indicators of their personal values: how does this candidate approach difficult situations? How do they balance tact and honesty? How will those complement what we're doing at the agency?

Once they're on board, we encourage that same open communication to continue. If anyone on our staff gets difficult feedback from a client, we want to know. If they have an idea for a new program, we'll run it through the filter of the company values together. And if they have a dilemma—especially one that has values implications—our doors are open. We never want our people to feel abandoned, or like they're left doing the difficult work alone. We never want them to face the temptation to cut corners because there's too much. We want to help each person feel a healthy self image and company image, and to be committed to the work they're doing.

Our employees are our eyes and ears, the true face of what we're doing. If we don't stay plugged into what they're saying and feeling, then we don't know what values are being shared with our customers.

Leaders share the spotlight. The trend recently has been for bigger, splashier, more attention-grabbing meetings. CEOs are getting on spotlighted stages and emceeing full, multi-media-powered shows, with cameras and big screens.

The problem with spotlights, though, is that they leave the audience in the dark, and can highlight *us-vs.-them* differences. If those on-stage meetings are the only time that an employee interacts with their CEO, it may come across as alienating, not motivational. When the show ends, the rank and file must still stumble along in the dark, not quite sure where they're going.

In this socially transparent age, we expect our leaders to be three-dimensional. That's because we want our leaders to be real people who represent our own real values. We want them to acknowledge us. We look for someone who shares the spotlight. We long for genuine recognition and appreciation.

The next time you're going to address your team or the entire staff, leave the slides at home, step off the stage, and get off the script. Take the time to publicly acknowledge the work of others, individually or as teams. Engage in town hall meetings. Invest in two-way video, so that you can see your far-flung employees, just as they see you. Don't hide in your corner office. Answer questions. Get face-to-face with as many people as possible. How do they define your corporate culture?

At our agency, one of the ways we've chosen to share the spotlight is to give our team the chance to publicly recognize each other. Honoring hard work and expressing genuine gratitude for contributions is a powerful tool for a leader to use. My partners and I emcee a monthly all-hands meeting, but we don't set the agenda. These are rewards meetings, and we're just the carnival barkers. Employees organize the time to reward their peers, and to draw out examples of recent work that reflect the company's values. It happens peer-to-peer, and it reinforces what's important. It brings the company's values to every employee and invests them in the outcome. When they're challenged to recognize values, they own them.

Leaders focus on the *why*. Remember the story I told you back in Chapter 3, about my father leading his soldiers in World War II? It's not enough to tell people where they're fighting; you have to help them believe in why they're fighting. And it has to be a compelling why, something that's worth getting out in front of and owning publicly.

A company's brand is only as important as its stories. Why are you making the product that you make? Why are you asking employees to come in day after day and give themselves to this business? Was your chain of pizza restaurants once a single store, where an immigrant baker shared the recipe his grandmother gave him? Did your accounting agency grow from a single, dedicated worker who was determined to tell the truth, no matter what it cost him?

In one well-publicized study, a psychology student named Adam Grant wanted to test the idea of what motivates people at work. He started a study at the donation-soliciting call center at his school, the University of Michigan. Like most dialing-for-dollars job, it was difficult and generally thankless; employees experienced a 93% rejection rate, even from their own alumni. Grant wondered if he could change that number by changing the attitudes of the employees. Since most of the donations that the callers were soliciting went to scholarships, Grant brought in a university scholarship student, who spent ten minutes describing to the call center workers how attending college had changed his life. He told his story, and then he left. The call center workers hit the phones again. Nothing else about their jobs had changed; they kept the same scripts and the same schedules. Their manager was instructed not to mention the scholarship recipient again.

A month later, the numbers showed that workers were spending 142% more time on the phone, and were successfully raising 171% more revenue. No employee incentive program had ever had that kind of effect. The employees couldn't even identify that it was the hearing the scholarship student's story that had changed things. They just knew that they were now more motivated.

Grant replicated the study five times with the same results: workers who understood some part of the story behind why they were acting—and could feel good about being a part of that—were more effective and successful.[61]

Do your employees know why they're working for you? When you're telling stories, don't just focus on the folklore of the past. What are the stories about what your brand is doing now? Celebrate the customers who are living your values. Recognize the unique moments where your brand is making a difference. In the Values Economy, you aren't just laying cable wires to increase bandwidth; you're offering a grandmother a chance to be part of her distant grandson's fifth birthday party via high-speed video conferencing.

A leader's first and biggest job is not to focus on the bottom line; it's to inspire their team of employees and customers with the vision of what they're doing together.

I firmly believe that most employees don't come to work every day wanting to do a bad job. They don't want to put in the least possible amount of effort. Instead, I believe that most people come to work wanting to do the best they can, but then they're sidelined. They're ignored. They're not trusted, and so they don't offer trust in return. Their enthusiasm is steadily, persistently, painfully cut away, to the point where they end up showing up just for the paycheck. Too many of them end up leaving their humanity at the door and convincing themselves that they're okay with mediocrity, or outright dishonesty, and investing themselves in everything but their vocation.

IF YOUR ORGANIZATION'S VALUES DON'T LINE UP

I'll admit it: it's easy for me to say that you should mirror your company's values, because I think that the values of my company are pretty terrific.

But that wasn't always the case. I lived through some atrocious behavior in my early career, working for a company that was trying to hold onto the wheeling-and-dealing, three-martini lunch lifestyle of the 1960s, and that had no interest in its employees or its customers. The greed was something so tangible I could feel it in the hallway. It pricked my conscience and clashed with values I didn't even know yet that I had. But I knew that something was wrong.

This has happened to most people at some point: they've found themselves in a professional culture that just doesn't fit with what they believe or who they want to be. They struggle with a desire to be human in a setting that just doesn't care about humanity.

Some of them stay too long, and they slip into a kind of Stockholm Syndrome, identifying and sympathizing with the very systems that hurt them. They "go along to get along," parroting the company line and following orders for so long that it starts to seem normal. They may get sucked into an ever-deepening pit of ethical grayness. Most of the managers at Enron and the auditors at Arthur Andersen probably didn't start out with the intention of defrauding investors or lying to government regulators. But when everyone around you is acting in a certain way, and justifying their behavior, it gets harder to remember your own values. Cutting corners to meet impossible expectations feels necessary. Overlooking a safety standard here, or a trust violation there, is justified by the bottom line. The talk at the water cooler is poisonous.

When and if they finally emerge from the rubble of a company that imploded under its own weight, those Stockholm Syndrome survivors seem dazed, blinking in the suddenly bright light. "How did I get here? Who have I become?"

This can happen to anyone from the most junior intern to the CEO of a company. There's always pressure from somewhere, and a temptation to slide into complacent values that will support someone's greed. But no one should stay in a poison place. If your workplace is slowly dying due to its values, take stock of your options.

If a place is truly poisonous, chances are that you're not the only one who sees it. Others, too, are struggling, but may not know how to address it, or may lack the courage to speak first.

If you are in a senior leadership position, or have been with a company long enough to have gathered seniority and respect, I believe you have the responsibility to speak up, and to try to lead the organization toward a better path. You're invested here, and you have the power to influence, at least in some way. I'm not suggesting that you turn over the conference room table and create a scene out of the movies. Organize your thoughts, and be sure that you can identify the specific areas where trust violations and complacent values have influenced the brand. Understand and articulate what the long-term consequences are. For example:

If we continue to use substandard material, our customers will find something better.

If we continue to cut our employees' benefits while maintaining our own, their dissatisfaction will influence our public approval.

If we continue to chase the next sale, without any clearly stated values, we will disappear in the sea of sameness.

If you're brave enough to suggest another path, others will follow.

If you are at an organization where the values violently collide with your own beliefs, and you're not in an influential leadership position, you have a choice. You can approach someone in management with an observation similar to what's above. Be specific about what you've seen, but don't cast blame. This isn't about pointing a finger at a specific person who has failed, but helping others see a much bigger, looming crisis. Again, the chances are that if you've seen a problem, others have as well, and they're just waiting for someone else to make the first move.

Your other option, of course, is to leave. That's what I did, as a young advertiser who just couldn't stomach being in the wrong culture anymore. With a few of my likeminded colleagues, I slipped out of that fancy office on a Friday afternoon, and on Monday morning we set up our own independent advertising agency. We were just wide-eyed novices in an empty room; we didn't even have a phone at first. (We gave potential clients the number of the pay phone on the corner—that was back in the day when there were pay phones—and had an intern stand next to it all day and answer if it rang.)

The CEO was furious, and called us "young, selfish fast-trackers devoid of team loyalty." On the contrary. We were deeply loyal to our own values, and to our vision of creating meaning instead of being shackled to a dying organization driven by the accounting department. It was one of the best decisions I ever made.

My personal values and purpose were worth more than my salary. I never doubted that choice. Twenty years later, my first employer was out of business and forgotten, and The Values Institute is earning the attention of businesses and researchers.

EIGHT

TESTING YOUR VALUES

How do you know if you're successfully communicating your values with your key stakeholders?

This isn't a trick question. It's one thing to identify your values and to commit to living them out in your personal life and in the workplace. But whether others correctly understand your efforts—and whether those efforts influence them in the ways you want—are different questions entirely. The ultimate goal is to achieve real trust.

Any social scientist will tell you that human impressions are fallible, and that objective, quantitative measurement is an important part of considering the effectiveness of an idea or program. In our personal lives, we may feel like we're eating the right food and getting enough exercise, but the numbers on the scale or the readings from the blood tests offer the only consistent and unbiased interpretation of our behavior over time.

As we've seen, long-term workplace satisfaction and success come from relationships built on trust. But that's not an easy element to capture on a spreadsheet. You can't get an up-to-the-minute reading on how successfully you're communicating your values the way you can your current stock price or the number of units shipped last quarter.

Or can you?

How do you measure something as nebulous as the development of trust, which we already know builds slowly, over time? How can you tell if your employees are more engaged this year than last? Are your customers responding to the values messaging that you're sharing?

Just as our closest personal relationships need constant nurturing and regular check-ins, trustworthy brands need to nurture their relationships with their customers by keeping vigilant watch over their performance and evaluating their success.

THE PYRAMID OF TRUST

To help in this endeavor, The Values Institute created what we call the Pyramid of Trust, which incorporates five distinct areas of satisfaction in personal and brand relationships. These "5 C's" were compiled and extracted from years of our own research and inspired by other leading organizations like J.D. Power and Associates, Steven Covey, Simon Sinek, and the International Association of Business Communicators (IABC), studying personal and corporate trust. Each element in the Pyramid can be broken down, tracked, and measured individually, allowing a brand to objectively see where they are succeeding in both employee and public perception, and whether that impression is growing or slipping over time.

However, before we start to explore how to measure each area, I want to stress that the real benefit of the Pyramid of Trust is not that it gives you words to dissect, track, and report. The five elements—Competence,

Consistency, Concern, Candor, and Connection—should not be separated from one another in the final analysis, because they are individual stages of a single journey toward the ultimate goal: trust. The connections between the elements, and what those reveal about how a company or individual expresses their values, are as important as the elements themselves.

Your goal, as a brand, shouldn't be to improve your Candor score; it should be to understand how your candor is helping you distinguish your brand's identity and achieve the ultimate relational outcomes of loyalty, satisfaction, and even advocacy. That is where genuine trust, and long-time commitment, happen.

As you approach this, it's also important to remember that it's not an easy process to get here; this isn't a maze or a flat race with a series of hurdles to jump. We designed the Pyramid of Trust as a steep-sided mountain on purpose, to demonstrate that it takes effort to get to the top. The farther into this journey you get, the more limited are the opportunities to reach that higher ground of genuine connectedness, and the risks are higher. However, as we'll see, so are the payoffs.

To approach the pyramid, it may help to first remember another series that's also represented by a pyramid: Maslow's Hierarchy of Needs, which posits that human motivations begin with certain base requirements, which must be met before a person will start to look for other, higher experiences of satisfaction and self actualization.[62]

Our pyramid works similarly. The two elements that make up the base levels of trust—Competence and Consistency are the foundations of every brand's trust relationship, demonstrated in the way that it acts and reacts within its sphere of influence on a daily basis. The middle of the pyramid finds Concern and Candor which begin to transcend mere functional abilities adding more emotionally charged "glue" to relationships. The top of the triangle—Connection—represents the ultimate goal, and the place where the values-driven magic happens.

As we saw in Chapter 3, the very least that a customer requires from a brand in order to have a positive impression is Competency and Consistency. These make up the base of our pyramid, the Rational factors. A brand must be able to meet its commitments and perform the basics well before customers will view them with any satisfaction. However, as the global economy provides us with more choices and basic security, most people won't consider competency and consistency enough to form genuine bonds and Identification-level trust with a brand.

Unfortunately, most brands live here at the bottom of the pyramid, without any investment in a deeper connection. These brands don't stand out. Their employees and customers may not know why they exist, and at the end of the day, they're still left with that general sense of "is this all there is?"

Built onto that are two Emotional elements of trust: Concern and Candor. Once a brand has established itself as worthy of that calculus-based trust we described in Chapter 2, it must also demonstrate respect for the people in its sphere of influence. Concern and candor in a brand are comparable to the honesty, authenticity, and open communication that benefit our interpersonal relationships. It's the place where a customer or employee can perceive that they're more than another sale or a dollar figure on the bottom line.

This idea of perception is important. A CEO may lie awake at night, worrying about how she will continue to meet her payroll in an economic downturn or what she will say publicly about a sensitive compromise she had to make with a vendor. A product engineer may pore over feedback from early test groups to make sure a product addresses all of their concerns. But those are invisible to most people. Those behaviors are part of how a company lives out its values, but the measurable element is how a brand *publicly demonstrates* its commitment to values.

Eventually, with time, effort, and a commitment to shared values, a brand can reach the tip of the pyramid with Connection. This is the ultimate piece that we look for; it's the place where the brand and the consumer, or the employer and the employee, actually act together, and on behalf of one another. Connection is the place where a brand stands out in the sea of sameness; it's the self actualization goal described by Maslow.

Brands aren't automatically given connection. In fact, our annual Most Trusted Brands surveys reveal that Connection is a huge stumbling block for most companies. Remember, that identification-level trust is rare, and offered only after time. Brands must earn it as they demonstrate trust and shared values over time and multiple interactions. But the old saw is true: familiarity can also build contempt. The key, according to our research, is for brands to make sure that they seize each opportunity to make customers feel valued, instead of allowing our disappointment to accumulate, fester, and ultimately drive us into the arms of a competitor. Sometimes it's a detail as simple as remembering our names that can make the difference in our satisfaction and loyalty.

Yet connection can't happen without everything that supports it. If a stakeholder doesn't feel that you'll do what you say you will, and will respect them in the process, there's no reason to offer you any of their limited amount of loyalty and trust. Brands find themselves without the advocacy of loyal customers, and employees find themselves burning out, constantly struggling to achieve the base levels of business with no relational payoff. The messaging and experience that happens within the category of Connection must be consistent with what's happening internally, at the base, or the entire effort might sink.

Another way to think about the Pyramid of Trust is as an iceberg. The base—the four areas that represent the rational and emotional needs—exist below the surface of a customer's experience. A business has a responsibility to provide them, but the customer has no role in how they work. Connection, on the other hand, is the higher ground that rises above the waterline. It's the place where the customer and the company, or the employer and the employee, must both be engaged.

There's nothing benign about Connection. When a person earns an identification level of trust, they're rewarded with a satisfying, thriving relationship. That's because you won't find yourself standing on the pinnacle of the mountain alone. Connection demands a response, and a natural expression that comes back to you from the relationships you've established. The relationship, in many cases, stops being about the customer and the company. Instead, lines blur and it becomes a relationship of *community*, where each party provides a tool that the other needs in order to fulfill their shared goals.

When a business earns its connection to those around it—when it earns the deepest levels of *trust*—the business is rewarded not only with financial stability and growth, but with the deeper, more intangible elements of **loyalty**, **satisfaction**, and **advocacy**. When you have lived out your values on a daily basis, your customers and your employees become your ambassadors. Your sales force will expand exponentially. Your goodwill and good reputation will magnify. You reach the peak of trust.

This point of Connection is the true higher ground that will bring you, wherever you are as you read this book, to the place where you thrive instead of merely surviving. This path to trust is the ultimate path to your own satisfaction.

It's a hard journey, but the results are so worth it.

MEASURING YOUR PLACE ON THE PYRAMID

A friend of mine went to the doctor recently because she felt "off." There was no one specific symptom she could point to, but she knew her energy was down, and her body wasn't acting the way it normally did. The doctor ordered a series of blood tests, and the results gave them the clear, concrete data they needed to turn into an actual diagnosis that they could address.

Taking stock of your place on the Trust Pyramid has a similar remedy. While the journey toward trust is best addressed from a holistic perspective, taking a formal measurement of each of the five elements of trust is what gives business leaders a snapshot of what's working and what still needs work. Are there misperceptions that need to be addressed? Is there an area of the business that's falling short? Are your values reaching your most important stakeholders?

The only way to find out is to ask.

To accurately measure and track the 5 Cs over time, a business needs an objective system of gathering information and feedback from its stakeholders: its employees and its customers. Using simple online tools, we've put together a barometer of public perception to really identify where a brand is thriving, and where it's struggling.

But even if you're not ready for a special survey, there are ways for you to gather solid data, uncover insights or correlations, and review how much trust you've actually earned. Let's take a closer look.

Competency

Are you providing the service or product that you promised?

If Patagonia doesn't make great sweaters, then their commitment to environmental protection and the transparency in which they track the origin of their materials is irrelevant.

Competence measures a brand's quality and capacity to provide what people want and need. When we study the competence of a business, we look at the company's operational efficiency and their responsiveness to feedback, as well as the brand's capability to achieve what they promise. For example, if you run a hotel, do your customers perceive that you have a smooth check-in process, clean rooms, and a trustworthy billing process? If you're selling a mobile app, do users enjoy it? In either case, are there bugs (literal or electronic) affecting the customer's experience?

Are employees trained and capable of providing what customers expect? One of the primary indicators of competence is employee readiness. Our values can only truly be lived out through an energized, well-trained, and highly skilled workforce. Each employee must have the tools they need to do their job with excellence.

Competence may seem like a given, but there are plenty of reasons why a brand may struggle at the basic level. We meet a lot of young, idealistic companies with great intentions, but they falter with their customers because they haven't fully developed their product offerings or clearly defined their services. Customers feel let down when the actual interaction doesn't live up to the hype. And on the other end, there are plenty of older companies that have gotten sloppy with their business practices, or that offer outdated products or technology that hamstring their workers. If your customer isn't interested in what you offer—or worse, actively dislikes the experience that they have with you—then they'll never linger long enough to understand what you stand for.

Consistency

Are you dependable? Do your actions reflect your values?

You can't measure trust episodically. If the behavior of a friend, a spouse, a boss, or coworker is inconsistent—if they show up as Dr. Jekyll one day and Mr. Hyde the next—we tend to withdraw from the relationship rather than wade in deeper. It's not enough for Zappos to "wow" one person, but then leave hundreds of others on hold. You can't shower your employees with perks and benefits when the economy is strong and then pull back when things get tough, but expect the same level of loyalty. Organizational trust is built as a daily endeavor and ongoing process.

Consistency is a measure of a brand's stability and reliability. It is tied directly to organizational structure. We gauge consistency by asking customers if the company and its employees follow through with what they say. Do they stand behind their commitments? And in an increasingly transparent marketplace, does the customer perceive that the way that the brand approaches its everyday actions and behavior reflects its values?

Internally, we look at whether there are functional barriers that contradict a company's values and hamper their ability to provide a consistent experience. Antiquated customer relationship management tools, for example, or outdated IT systems can directly contradict a business' stated value on efficiency. High staff turnover can affect a customer's experience.

A second level of consistency is the idea that brands change over time. When we study an organization's position with its customers, we always recommend that they go through the process annually, to track movement over time. Trust takes time to develop, and customers may not immediately react to new initiatives or messages. You can only see movement in a relationship if you stop to take stock more than once. On the flip side, in a fast-moving global culture, customers' expectations change along with the competition. What was working three years ago may be obsolete now—a lesson that many brands learned when they were late to embrace social media and lost customers to other, more nimble organizations.

Concern

Are you publicly invested in your customers and employees? How do show you genuinely care?

When the CEO of Starbucks repeatedly and passionately credits his store's success to its employees, and then backs up the statement by increasing benefits and organizing all-expense-paid leadership conferences for local store managers, we see his concern. When a national food chain like Chipotle pulls carnitas from most of its restaurant menus because it can't source enough sustainably raised and humanely treated pork, we see it living up to its value of "food with integrity."

Concern measures whether a brand or business is *perceived* as respecting and caring about its customers, clients, and employees. When we survey, we ask questions like "How well does the company listen (even when it involves complaints or bad news)?" and "How do they demonstrate that they care?"

Concern is typically transmitted through an organization's non-business-related interactions with both its employees and customers, and its public role within its community. By clearly focusing on relationships and human needs more than the bottom line or the next transaction, a business has the opportunity to leverage its values in new and meaningful ways. Concern creates bonds among individuals and adds a social purpose to a company's reason to exist. These acts of shared loyalty and commitment are what drive the Concern numbers, and show a brand's stakeholders what it really values.

Candor

Are you honest?

When a company like Google announces that its mission is simply "don't be evil," its customers react to the transparency and simplicity of the message—and then they expect the company to live up to its commitment. When a brand admits, without excuses, its responsibility in a mistake, we react generously to their honesty. Positively impacting lives begins with demonstrating that your brand cares more about the relationship than the transaction.

Candor is the measure of how the public perceives the genuineness and transparency of a brand. How honest and frank is the communication? How open and transparent is the company? Does the customer know how they make decisions? Do employees feel like they have been trusted with the truth about what happens behind closed doors, and are told why decisions are made? Research constantly shows that the trust gap between senior management and employees hinges on a perceived lack of open and honest communication.

Beyond these key trust requirements, we also assess if the company values their customer relationships and rewards loyalty.

Companies that struggle with their candor scores are often perceived as adding unnecessary layers of complexity to even the simplest of tasks. This is most often the case in those areas which consumers are least equipped to understand on our own and must rely on experts, like healthcare, automotive services, and computers. When customers struggle through endless phone trees or can't understand the bills that are sent to them, that affects a brand's Candor scores. In a vacuum of silence from a company's leadership, the public is left to "fill in the blanks" with whatever gossip or assumptions they have. Businesses that appear to be hiding their decision processes or shielding their accounting practices, we wonder what else they're hiding.

Candor feels like it should be an easy dimension for a brand to implement—just be more honest—but it often rubs against long traditions of privacy and concern. Layers of bureaucracy must be pushed aside. Cultures of self-protection must be changed. Employees must be trusted.

The effort consistently shows itself to be worth the short-term struggles. According to the data, candor is the deciding factor when our trust is split among brands with which we're connected. When we like and trust multiple brands within a category, the most transparent contender wins.

Connection

Do your customers feel like they have a personal relationship with you?

The potent combination of rational and emotive trust factors builds up to the one dimension of self actualization which requires the participation of customer: connection.

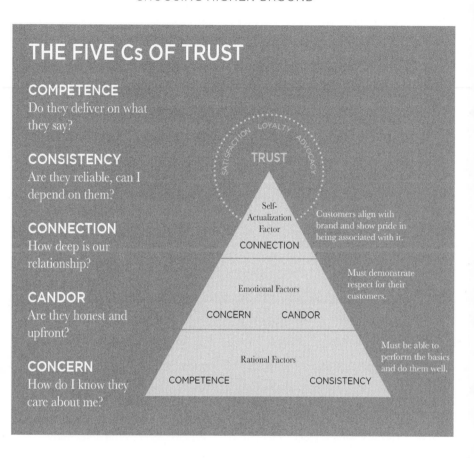

THE FIVE Cs OF TRUST

COMPETENCE
Do they deliver on what they say?

CONSISTENCY
Are they reliable, can I depend on them?

CONNECTION
How deep is our relationship?

CANDOR
Are they honest and upfront?

CONCERN
How do I know they care about me?

TRUST

SATISFACTION LOYALTY ADVOCACY

Self-Actualization Factor
CONNECTION

Customers align with brand and show pride in being associated with it.

Emotional Factors
CONCERN   CANDOR

Must demonstrate respect for their customers.

Rational Factors
COMPETENCE   CONSISTENCY

Must be able to perform the basics and do them well.

Connection is the measure of how well brands identify with the relationships they value most. It is all about creating emotional engagement. When we study a brand's connection measurements, we measure how well customers feel like they are aligned with a brand and show pride in being associated with it. We also look at the depth, duration, and anticipated longevity of a relationship. Does the customer feel connected to the people and company behind the brand? And beyond the transaction, we evaluate the shared values, views, and opinions at work in the relationship.

149

All of the rational and emotional factors of measurement look at what a brand is actively doing to distinguish themselves. But connection turns the camera around and measures how customers are responding. Do they feel the sense of identity and belonging?

When a person feels that their values align with those of a brand, to the point where we experience a sense of loyalty and inclusion in a "family," we become proud advocates for the brand, and our dedication to it remains steadfast. Connection reveals itself in the relationships where the brand name supersedes the action itself: connected customers are Harley riders instead of motorcycle riders, or MacBook users instead of laptop users.

Connection is the hardest piece of the trust puzzle to pin down, because there's no specific way to build it or improve it. Connection is a natural extension of all of the other things that are part of trust, combined with an even-less-tangible attitude that the customer and the brand are both seeking the same things. But it's important to remember that connection is also a conscious decision; it doesn't "just happen" by chance, but comes only through a deliberate effort to seek a lasting, meaningful relationship.

That kind of identification-level trust and commitment demands a response from the customer; they can't just be consumers of a product anymore. If the brand is going to be this invested, then the customer feels called to a certain loyalty, as well.

A connected customer will seek out your brand, even when a competitor is cheaper or more convenient. They'll tell their friends about their experiences and advocate on your behalf. They'll become your ambassadors and models.

Connection is the hardest trust value for a brand to achieve, because it depends on the foundation of all four other dimensions. But as we've seen, it also comes with the greatest rewards possible. If even one of these dimensions weakens, the pyramid falls out of balance, and connection is difficult to maintain or build. However, it's also clearly the most powerful. Without it, trust is fleeting.

A LIFETIME COMMITMENT

My former business partner, Mandi Dossin, has a saying, "The vines have a way of growing back." She was absolutely right. It's human nature to become complacent once the initial excitement of a new relationship or project fades. Without hard data to show us reality, we may overemphasize the impact of our past efforts, or expect that early enthusiasm about our values projects will continue, unchanged.

In fact, the journey to build lasting relationships and trust is just that—a journey. We must constantly take stock of where we are now and what conditions we're facing. Things do change, and if we leave our commitments untended, and unmeasured, we open the door for competitive intrusion. Just look at what happened to former giants like Nokia, PanAm, Borders, Blockbuster, and even Woolworths—brands we once couldn't imagine being without, but that barely left a mark when they disappeared.

NINE

WHERE ARE YOUR VALUES
IN A CRISIS?

Mary Barra had been working toward this job for her whole life. The daughter of an auto worker, she grew up in Detroit and started working for GM when she was just eighteen. She went to school for engineering and mechanics on a GM scholarship and moved up through the ranks until finally, in December 2013, she drew worldwide attention when she was promoted to CEO and became the first female chief executive of a major American automaker. According to *Forbes* Magazine, Barra became the seventh most powerful woman in the world overnight.

But she drew even more headlines three months later, when reports surfaced showing that for more than a decade, GM had been manufacturing cars with a defective ignition switch. At least thirteen people had died. And to make it even worse, there was evidence that GM staff had known about the problem but failed to act, possibly because of the cost and impact of a recall. No one was willing to be the one who blew the whistle and faced responsibility. A deadly problem was shuffled from one committee to another, buried in reports and avoided like a hot potato.

The report was a devastating indictment. The classic American company that claimed values of safety and quality was actually drowning in a culture that shirked accountability and couldn't see the bigger picture.

Everyone agreed that Barra wasn't responsible for the conspiracy; she had been working in a different department and wasn't privy to the ignition switch reports. But she was left holding the ball when it became public.

At some point in every brand's existence, a crisis will hit. It may come from something uncontrollable, like a natural disaster, or you may be faced with the fallout from a mistake, a customer complaint, or a painful trust violation from a colleague or partner. Some crises, like the GM recall, build for years and involve many people and layers of complexity. Others erupt almost instantly, when a single, ill-thought-out comment on social media or in an interview turns into a PR nightmare.

You can't avoid every crisis. But, as we've learned, your values can help you successfully weather one.

WHAT'S YOUR TRACK RECORD?

Martin Luther King, Jr. said, "The ultimate measure of a man is not where he stands in moments of comfort and convenience, but where he stands at times of challenge and controversy." The same is true for brands and businesses.

It's easy to post a list of values on your website. It's harder, for some, to live them out every day. And the times we see the disparity most is when things go wrong. When a brand finds itself caught in the harsh glare of the public spotlight, customers find out what values truly drive a company, and the individuals behind it.

For GM, that insight was painful. Instead of an American company that was "passionate about earning customers for life," we saw a bureaucratic, bloated, isolated culture that protected jobs and reputations at all costs—even at the expense of their customers' lives.

But GM is certainly not alone. Plenty of companies reveal the disparity between what they say and what they do when a crisis strikes. Sure, a business may claim to stand for community or quality, but when there's a lawsuit, individuals turn on each other and any vendor or associate within reach. When the money gets tight, not many executives give up their salaries and perks before they start to cut jobs and worker benefits.

At the same time, we've seen customers abandon a brand when its reputation takes a hit. Donations to a charity dry up when there are allegations of impropriety. Customers find another place to shop when a business is buried in stories of poor labor practices. We live in a time when we have options, and we don't need to associate with those who don't share what we believe.

On the other hand, for every celebrity who fell from grace or business that dissolved, we've also seen remarkable stories of comeback and redemption. Brands can come out stronger after a potentially dangerous revelation. The additional exposure can reveal something that draws people in, rather than push them away.

What makes the difference? According to our research, much of it comes down to human nature, and that innate desire for relationships that we all share. Humans are prone to forgiveness. We rebuild relationships that falter. We accept apologies and move forward.

How can you tackle a trust violation or other crisis in your own workplace, and use it as an opportunity to build a brand, rather than destroy it?

The first thing that we recognized after studying dozens of businesses in crisis is that a reputation that survives a crisis is built on more than that single episode. If you already have a relationship with customers, they are more likely to stand by you and offer grace after a product failure or an act of inconsistent behavior. You may lose some of their trust and find yourself once again working through those early levels of calculus-based evaluations of every action, and it can take years to build it back, but you're not abandoned.

We see this in our personal relationships. Some marriages survive infidelity, and parents and children reconcile after long years of strained relationships. There's so much equity built into the relationship that we can see past one particular, painful episode and invest in the person as a whole.

Legacies are built over time, and as we've seen, trust is built on a continuum. But shallow relationships are easy to shed. It's easy to walk away from an imperfect partner after a single date, and much harder after twenty years of marriage. The best way for your business to weather a crisis is to bank years of positive interactions and loads of trust before anything happens. Building a relationship with your customers offers your brand an impenetrable shield of protection. If a crisis is an anomaly, we are more likely to forgive. If it is a pattern, we will walk away.

Perhaps no case in recent memory reflects that more clearly than Lance Armstrong. As a professional road racing cyclist, for years he lived in the shadow of rumored substance abuse. He steadfastly and emotionally denied the claims, and his fans believed him. We—and I count myself among them—were drawn to the story of the American hero and cancer survivor who came back to beat the odds, time after time. We donated to his

Livestrong Foundation, bought his cycling jerseys, and cheered him on as he won a record seven Tour de France competitions. We felt like we knew Lance Armstrong, and connected with his powerful story of overcoming obstacles. We had deep feelings for the Armstrong brand. Measured according to the trust scale we talked about in Chapter 2, many of Armstrong's fans probably felt like they had an identification level of trust with him. We knew him well… or so we thought.

Except, of course, it was all a lie. The evidence mounted, witnesses came forward, and in 2012 the U.S. Anti-Doping Agency issued a lifetime ban from professional cycling based on evidence that Armstrong had engaged in illegal performance-enhancing practices. A few months after that, in an interview with Oprah Winfrey, Armstrong changed his story and admitted that he had been doping throughout his career.

The damage was near total. His sponsors dropped him. He was stripped of his titles. He had to step down from the Livestrong Foundation. His approval ratings plummeted to the single digits. A man who was once one of the most trusted and admired athletes in the country came crashing back down the trust pyramid to, at best, a deterrence level.

Armstrong had spent decades demonstrating competence and consistency. His cancer experiences and dedication to the Livestrong charity made a strong impression of concern. And it certainly looked like he was connecting with his customers—his fans, his sponsors, his teammates, his employees. But it all fell apart because of his failure of candor. His values proved to be false. And that, probably even more than the original sin, was his downfall.

A history of relationship is important, but our studies show that how you handle a crisis when it occurs also says a lot about your values. When faced with something potentially damaging, there are specific guiding principles that can help you maintain trust:

Trust depends on *immediate* honesty. Social researcher Brenè Brown studies human connections. In a popular TED talk on vulnerability, she offers her own take on values and honesty:

"We pretend that what we do doesn't have an effect on people. We do that in our personal lives. We do that corporately—whether it's a bailout, an oil spill, a recall—we pretend like what we're doing doesn't have a huge impact on other people. I would say to companies, this is not our first rodeo, people. We just need you to be authentic and real and say, 'We're sorry. We'll fix it.'"[63]

When stuff hits the fan, what's your first response? Do you try to deny it, or pass the blame? Or do you tackle it head on?

There is a human temptation to avoid *conflict*. We don't want to face the problem. We may not be intentionally trying to hurt anyone else, or to cheat, or to break the foundational rules of human interactions. We just don't want to get our hands messy, and we hope the problem will go away on its own. That's what it appears GM did. Everyone passed the responsibility of the ignition switches off to someone else. No one stepped forward to say "We're sorry. We'll fix it."

The darker side of dishonesty comes from those who appear to just not care about other people or the impact of their actions. They are the ones who are actively lying, denying, and trying to avoid *consequences*. They continue to make hurtful decisions until they are forced to stop. That's what Lance Armstrong did.

Either way, trying to avoid a crisis once it's started is the worst possible thing you can do to protect your reputation and preserve your relationships. The collapse of trust often comes because of a cover-up, not the initial violation.

Brands crumble under the weight of secrets and dishonesty. But we forgive someone who immediately admits a mistake and genuinely apologizes.

On Valentine's Day 2007, an ice storm swept across the northeast United States and halted air traffic. The economy carrier JetBlue was hit particularly hard. Passengers sat in unheated, unsanitary planes on the runways of its hub at New York's JFK airport for hours. The delays completely disrupted JetBlue's tight schedule of moving airplanes and crew around the country, and over the following days more than 1,000 flights were canceled. The company's innovative but untested reservation system collapsed when so many people needed to rebook at the same time. Many travelers didn't get to their final destination for days.

The story made national news and stayed there. Public opinion started to turn on the airline, which had made "bringing humanity back to air travel" its guiding value. This could have crippled the young company. But instead, JetBlue tackled the crisis head-on. They doubled down on that value of honoring their customers by jumping out in front of the story.

On February 19, then-CEO David Neeleman posted a video on YouTube and apologized. It wasn't fancy or professionally produced; it's just two and a half minutes of a guy in a wrinkled shirt and a clip-on microphone, looking tired and talking to the camera. He fumbles his words at times, but it makes his message seem even more authentic. Neeleman doesn't blame the weather, or the forecasters who'd promised that the sleet would turn to rain, or the airport tower controllers who couldn't coordinate getting the stranded planes back to open gates. Instead, he acknowledges that this has been "the most difficult time in our history." He says that his company let passengers down, and he starts to talk about how he will make it right.

"As all challenges when they come your way, there are a couple of things that you can do: you can ignore it and pretend like it was an aberration. Or you can do an examination and determine if there's something that you can do internally to make sure that that never happens again."[64]

And then he explains what JetBlue will do to make it better, starting with refunds and immediate plans for better emergency staffing. Two days later, JetBlue introduced a groundbreaking "Customer Bill of Rights," which laid out a policy of compensation and redress for any JetBlue passenger who faced future operational failures.

An event that could have sunk the company turned into a public relations triumph. JetBlue passengers remained loyal, even ranking the carrier first among low-cost carriers that year and every year since in the influential J.D. Power North America Airline Satisfaction Survey.

In a crisis, time matters. Your first response needs to respect your customer and, when appropriate, take responsibility for making things right. Don't let your corporate conscience hide behind the fear of conflict or consequences.

Trust depends on transparency. It's one thing to say you're sorry. It's another to take the steps to build a relationship again. For a brand to make its way back to its values, it must make a visible, open effort to reconnect with key supporters.

In 2009, Domino's Pizza was already one of the largest and most popular pizza chains in the United States, with almost 9,000 restaurants around the world. But then, on a quiet Sunday night in a small town in North Carolina, two local franchise employees made a prank video that showed them doing some pretty offensive things to a pizza, supposedly for an unsuspecting customer. The video went viral within hours. Before the corporate communications team at Domino's succeeded in having the video pulled three days later, it had more than one million views. The story was widely covered in the media. And the worst part was that most people didn't realize it was a hoax.

The company's reputation took a huge hit. The impression of the brand went from positive to negative. One national survey from HCD Research showed that 65% of respondents said that they were less likely to visit or order from Domino's Pizza after viewing the video. Long-time customers told the brand that they were considering abandoning it for a competitor.[65]

Domino's moved relatively quickly to fire the employees, expose the hoax, and pull the video. But that didn't change the tide of opinion. They needed to counter the shift in public impression, and to regain trust. And that plan, they decided, needed to be just as visible as the embarrassing trust violation that threw them into the spotlight. Domino's needed customers to see everything that the company was doing to ensure the quality of the product.

The corporate marketing department launched a series of high-visibility projects: in 2010, a new ad campaign featuring CEO Patrick Doyle acknowledged, on camera, that customers complained about the disappointing taste of their pizzas. They launched an 18-month overhaul of the menu, called The Pizza Turnaround, and promised new recipes for everything from the sauce to the topping mixtures, as well as the crust, which one focus group member famously said tasted "like cardboard."

It seemed like a daring, risky thing to do; what kind of CEO goes out and acknowledges that their product is sub-par? How could they avoid that becoming the sound bite? But customers loved it. They wanted that kind of honesty. Domino's Chief Marketing Officer, Russell Weiner, explained in an interview with *Forbes*:

"Consumers were just looking for people to stop lying to them, stop ripping them off and just be truthful and transparent. That was a societal finding, not specifically related to pizza, obviously. But we felt that if we could make it part of our brand strategy, our communication would help us take off because it was something that wasn't just applicable to pizza consumers, it was applicable to everybody."[66]

Domino's wasn't done yet. In 2011, they rented an electronic billboard in Times Square and shared real-time reviews of customer comments submitted through their website. They promised that "barring profanity and irrelevant rants," no comments would be excluded, no matter how negative. In 2013, they launched a live-video stream directly from some franchise pizza kitchens, so that customers at home could watch their pizzas being made. That service evolved into the Domino's Track, where every customer who orders online can now track, in real time, the progress of their pizza from order to delivery.

The efforts at transparency have paid off. When the crisis happened, Domino's stock price was struggling at $7 a share. Today, it's more than $100.

An apology and responsibility is an important first step. But to rebuild a damaged reputation, your brand needs to invite customers to see the rehabilitation in "real time." They won't trust what they can't see, but they will respect the risk that comes with real honesty.

Trust depends on a genuine interest in making things right. Crisis control that's based on relationships and influential values isn't about self protection. It's not defensive, and it doesn't hide. When we're in a giving, unselfish relationship with someone, we want to make sure that they're cared for. That's more than the basic desire to not hurt them, or to comply with the regulations that govern how we must treat them. It's about actively trying to help, even when there's a personal sacrifice involved.

One of the classic cases of corporate crisis management comes from the days before social media or cable news. In 1982, an unknown perpetrator laced Tylenol pain relief pills in the Chicago area with cyanide. Seven people died. The sensational story made national news.

Johnson & Johnson, the maker of Tylenol, reacted quickly. Internally, they formed a task force to lead the response. Chairman James Burke offered two directives: first, "How do we protect the people?" And then, *after that was answered*, "How do we save the product?"[67] From the first hours, the company focused first on the relationship with the customers.

They set up a 24-hour-a-day phone hotline to answer customer questions, and they recalled *every* bottle of Tylenol from *every* store shelf in the country. They committed to developing a tamper-proof seal that would protect future bottles. Their leaders got in front of TV cameras and gave as many media interviews as possible, telling people not to use their product until the safety could be verified.

No one made them do this. Johnson & Johnson didn't wait for government regulators or prosecutors to step in and mandate their behavior. Their reaction wasn't about being compliant. It was about being right, and honoring their relationship with their customers.

More than thirty years later, we don't see much of that proactive service anymore. Brands fall back on compliance rather than influence. They wait for the government to tell them what they have to do, instead of doing what's right.

Values-driven crisis management gets in front of an issue by proactively seeking to make things right. The lawyers often don't like it. They advise restraint, and not offering anything before it's required. They worry that an acknowledgment, or an apology, can be used against a brand in an eventual, perhaps inevitable lawsuit. Like some of the middle managers at GM, they try to weigh the cost of an admission of guilt against the cost of an acknowledgment.

But trust isn't built on a cost-benefit spreadsheet. Customers are looking for leadership, not safe answers. They are judging whether a brand lives up to its values.

This is controversial. This is countercultural. Business no longer defaults to telling the truth. But that's who we are as human beings. We're naturally drawn to honesty and transparency and caring for others. And so we, as individuals, suffer when our desires are in conflict with the behavior we see around us. If we could bring those back into balance, we rediscover what we were naturally designed for, and we flourish.

No brand is ever fully beyond repair. Mary Barra, in her first year as CEO of GM, made a number of important decisions and acted decisively to address the problems, not just of the defective switches, but of the culture that allowed them to happen.

She recalled more than a million cars, including some that are no longer even produced. But more surprising to her employees was that she set out to change the company's culture. "In the past," she told a Congressional panel, "we had more of a cost culture, and now we have a customer culture that focuses on safety and quality."

She fired the people who should have known about the ignition switch problem and the cover-up. She changed the way that safety concerns were reported. And she instituted a new culture, leading by example, of directness, transparency, and candor. When she introduced the new structure to GM employees, she said, "I'm not *asking* people to do it. It's a requirement—not only that they hold themselves accountable to do it, but they hold each other accountable. That's the message I've delivered and will continue to drive through the whole organization. This is not optional."[68]

TEN

LOOKING FORWARD

The twentieth century was a time of unprecedented growth: companies merged, grew, and explored a global marketplace. Profits soared. Consumers with resources and access they'd never experienced before drove a marketplace of *stuff*, the bigger the better.

The twenty-first century has proven to be a very different place. Our stuff doesn't make us happy anymore. Our leaders have proven untrustworthy. We've been wounded and betrayed.

And we've started looking for answers elsewhere. In difficult times, we've pulled back to relationships, to purpose, and, yes, to shared values.

Our time and energy are limited. We don't want to share them with just anyone; we want to share ourselves with those who will help make our world a better place in some way. And so, when surrounded by more brands than we can conceive, let alone consume, we choose to align ourselves with brands that are distinguished with a purpose and a vision. Maybe they're saving the environment. Maybe they're returning to a family-focused way of life. Maybe they're challenging others to have fun.

Whatever it is, the brands that are thriving today and are setting themselves up for the future have convinced us that they care about us as people, not just as consumers. They've joined us in the Values Economy. And their power and influence will just keep growing.

This isn't something that you can ignore. If you keep following the old rules of chasing profit above all, that dysfunction that's cracking the base of your company will continue to grow. Those customers will continue to be apathetic and easily wooed away. Those employees will continue to skirt by on as little as possible.

The solution to your dilemma is to stop mimicking what your competitors are doing, and start doing what your heart and conscience say is right. The Values Economy isn't a fad, and it isn't something that will pass. This move toward a purpose-driven experience is our cultural response to an over commoditized, over saturated commercial world, and it will only continue to grow.

As we look to the future, this is what we can expect:

Social consciousness will become the great differentiator between successful and unsuccessful organizations. Businesses that continue to abuse their employees, ignore their customers, and damage the environment will be increasingly alienated and irrelevant.

Investors, voters, and customers alike will start to look at a brand's demonstrated values as an indicator of its health and long-term success. Decisions will no longer be made solely on short-term financial prospects. Success will not just be measured by thinking differently than other companies, but will be about caring more than other companies—about customers, about colleagues, about how the organization conducts itself in a world with endless temptations to cut corners and compromise values. One of the long-term goals of The Values Institute is to develop a Trust Index for all publicly traded companies, one that will help brokers and investors see the sustainability and long-term potential of a brand based on its commitment to its values.

Brands will concentrate on building "advocacy communities" to establish their place in areas beyond their immediate transactions. The world is an overwhelmingly big place, and the issues that face us can seem insurmountable. But as each brand chooses where to plant its values flag, they will draw those who share their passions and purposes and can start to see real change.

When your brand faces a crisis situation, having an advocate community means having people in your corner who will speak up for you when you feel your voice is not being heard. Advocates who share your company's values are quick to introduce your brand to their own network of trusted relationships— critically important as we've come to learn that people trust their peers' opinions on products more than they trust what corporations say about their own products. A fully-engaged advocate community also stands ready to come to your defense when it feels you've been misrepresented by an "outlier." This phenomenon is seen in case after case of an online community casting out brand detractors without the need for intervention from the brand itself.

Growth will come not from hostile takeovers or aggressive program expansions, but from efforts designed for sustainability and deepening relationships. The values a brand shares with its customers will expand to encompass new ideas and new opportunities that clearly fit within the shared values.

Trust will define the ultimate value of a brand. Financial performance will no longer be enough to create sustained growth and value. Businesses will need to invest more of themselves into being transparent, consistent advocates for their customers and the things that they care about. Trust will be recognized as a must have, not simply a nice to have. The corporate community will realize that trust is a source of sustainable competitive advantage. Few rivals will go the extra mile to earn trust. Because trust is casually ambiguous and socially complex it is very costly to imitate. It is also difficult for competitors to observe trust, and capabilities that cannot be observed are hard to replicate. Just as brands measure customer awareness and satisfaction today, more and more will make a "trust index" part of their regular evaluations in the future. Market analysts and investors will look closely at the ability of brands to earn satisfaction, loyalty and advocacy both internally and externally before investing or recommending to a client.

New businesses will enter the marketplace with a strong values identity already in place. A number of higher education business programs are now training their students to start every business plan with a statement of values. Some, such as California State University Fullerton, are partnering with think tanks like The Values Institute to develop a full values-driven curriculum. Before they've even thought about profit, the next generation is learning to identify what will truly distinguish them.

This is our future, and the young are leading us. One of the things that has really encouraged me, as I work with companies of every size, is seeing how the Millennials are changing the way we work. They are coming into the workplace seeking greater purpose in their business lives and they're holding their employers accountable to provide purpose over profit.

Our view of success will dramatically shift. Brands will move their focus of success from short-term gains and the bottom line to the long-term realization of a new, more satisfying finish line. Our next generation of leaders understands intuitively that success isn't measured by the number of years you work for a company, or the size of your 401(K). Their success is built on the size of their experiences, not the size of their paychecks. I can see a future where we will measure success not against our competitors or the size of our market share, but rather solely on our ability to achieve our "why" believing that all other rewards will follow.

Recently a colleague of mine was meeting with a healthcare senior management team. In the course of the conversation she asked who they considered their major competitor. Expecting to hear of a hospital in same market you can imagine her surprise when they paused and answered, "cancer." What an inspired response. The singular focus—the "why" of this organization, was to save the world from an insidious enemy—not to surpass other hospitals in the region or boost profit. Imagine a future filled with brands, each out to become the very best versions of themselves and as a result improving the lives of all they touch.

YOUR PLACE IN THE FUTURE

Steve Jobs was probably one of the earliest adopters of the Values Economy, before we even knew that's what we would call it. He was a man who stood by what he believed, and developed a company that was known as much for its commitment to innovation as any particular product. In 1993, in an interview with *The Wall Street Journal*, he famously said, "Being the richest man in the cemetery doesn't matter to me...Going to bed at night saying we've done something wonderful...that's what matters to me."

When you go to bed tonight, what do you want to say you've accomplished? Is it that you got through another mindless meeting? Is it that you added another few points to the stock price? Or is it that you did something of value, something that connected you with people who care about the same things?

While the last nine chapters have been focused primarily on corporate culture, organizational values, and the positive effects that a life lived in the Values Economy will have on the ultimate success on your company, there's something even more important to consider—the life-affirming effect that living a life of values will have on you personally.

The hard, meaningful work of the Values Economy comes with personal rewards. Are you struggling with the never-ending pressure to make the next sale, or those tired middle managers who have no idea why you're doing the things you're doing? A life in the Values Economy will regenerate you.

There's an inexplicable sense of freedom and joy that comes when your life is in sync, and your personal values are aligned with the values of your workplace, where you spend so much of your time and energy. Some call it flow. Others call it rhythm. Whatever you call it, I can promise you that it's real. It took me forty years of what I now refer to as my "preparation season," but today I'm experiencing a revival. Living and working in the Values Economy has given me an immense peace of mind, both professionally and personally, as I cast away the masks I've worn in the many environments I've worked in.

So what will it take for you to experience this same sense of revival? First, know that any ounce of change starts with you. You can't point at those other managers or employees who just don't get it. You can't keep compromising yourself in order to chase your competition. There's a thread that binds together the people who live values-driven lives—courage. The courage to lead with your heart. The courage to allow yourself to be vulnerable. The courage not give in to the cultural pressures that don't align with your values. The courage to take a risk.

The choice is yours. How do you want to spend the rest of your life?

I've said it often in this book, and I'll say it again: This is hard work. Learning to see the world through your own lens will take courage. Establishing values and redirecting an organization's focus to honor those values takes time, and effort, and some tough choices. You can't buy it. You can't avoid it. It's earned over time.

And the bigger the ship, the harder it is to turn. If your business has been moving in the wrong direction for some time, gather your patience and thick skin; it may take months, or even years, to get it back on track. You'll need to win over stakeholders, employees, and customers. You may need to let some things go that once seemed important.

The Values Economy is a long game approach. Profits may not flow in as fast in the short term. You may need to re-think how you see words like success and failure.

It takes a commitment to live out your values on a daily basis and provide a constant dialogue with your customers. But with each positive interaction, the bond grows stronger and eventually will create a barrier to competitive intrusion. You may not make as much as your competitor did this quarter, but you'll have a different kind of satisfaction if you've made a longer-term impact. And you'll be here long after your competitor burns their last bridge.

These aren't easy visions to swallow. It's hard to imagine changing the entire way we approach our work, and to let go of our old measures of success.

But if you're honest with yourself, you probably already know that what we're talked about on these pages is true. These goals of purpose, relationship, and trust are where our human natures draw us—to express them and to align with others who do the same.

Whether you're selling pizzas or printing presses, whether you're offering subscriptions or healthcare, your experience will be richer if it means something more than a number on a spreadsheet. Your corporate results will last if you're offering relationships instead of transactions, purpose more than profit, transparency instead of opacity, conviction over compliance, and advocacy instead of apathy.

The days of the anonymous producers are coming to an end. Customers have choices, and they choose to affiliate with those who have a better story than sale. Employees have choices, and they want to do something that matters.

And you have a choice, too. You don't have to keep running on the hamster wheel. You don't have to keep pushing aside the parts of you that are human while you're at work. This can all mean something much bigger.

Move past the constant tension of fear and faking it.

Choose your values and live them. Lead by example and with courage.

This is going to change you.

This is going to change the world around you.

If your business disappeared tomorrow, would anyone notice?

They will now.

NOTES

1. Benjamin Snyder, "Volkswagen's Diesel Cheating Could Cause 60 People To Die Early," *Fortune* (October 30, 2015): http://goo.gl/Na5m15

2. "Meaningful Brands Country Factsheet: USA," *Havas Media.* http://goo.gl/LJUVxG

3. Roberto A. Ferdman, "The Pay Gap Between CEOs And Workers Is Much Worse Than You Realize," *The Washington Post* (September 25, 2014)

4. "2014 Edelman Trust Barometer: Trust In Employee Engagement," *Edelman* (2014): http://goo.gl/qWV3Kf

5. David Woods, "Half Of Employees Don't Trust Their CEO Or Senior Managers—And A Quarter Don't Trust HR," *HR Magazine* (April 6, 2009): http://goo.gl/tqJp8i

6. Mitchell Ogisi, "Majority Worldwide Sees Widespread Corruption In Businesses," *Gallup* (May 10, 2012): http://goo.gl/h8Ukg2

7. "What Is Wrong With Your Human Resources Department Satisfaction Survey," *Chart Your Course International* (July 18, 2012): http://goo.gl/x32QBA

8. Dan Crim and Gerard Seijts, "What Engages Employees The Most Or, The Ten Cs of Employee Engagement," *Ivey Business Journal* (March/April 2006): http://goo.gl/g6Cn7Y

9. Bruce Horovitz, "Consumers: We Don't Need Our Stuff," *USA Today Money* (May 12, 2014) http://goo.gl/lQkLWN

10. Ryan Knutson and Theo Francis, "Basic Costs Squeeze Families," *Wall Street Journal* (December 1, 2014): http://goo.gl/Amh8nU

11. Joel Stein, "On Demand Economy," *TIME* (February 9, 2015)

12. "The Health Benefits Of Strong Relationships," *Harvard Health Publications* (December 1, 2010): http://goo.gl/5eVJcw

13. Lisa F. Berkman and Breslow Lester, *Health And Ways Of Living: The Alameda County Study* (New York: Oxford University Press, 1983). Quoted in Debra Umberson and Jennifer Karas Montez, "Social Relationships And Health: A Flashpoint For Health Policy," *Journal of Health and Social Behavior* 51/1 (2010): S54-S66.

14. "Looking Further With Ford: 13 Trends For 2013," *Ford Motor Company.* http://goo.gl/RlgmTP

15. Sree Rama Rao, "Types Of Trust In Organizational Relationships," *CiteMan.com* (July 12, 2008): http://goo.gl/SZayDs

16. Emily Steel and Ravi Somaiya, "Brian Williams Loses Lofty Spot On A Trustworthiness Scale," *The New York Times* (February 9, 2015)

17. NBC *Nightly News,* "Trust," *YouTube* (December 1, 2014): https://goo.gl/gJWqtL

18. Kathryn Dill, "The 10 Happiest Retailers To Work For In 2014," *Forbes* (November 25, 2014): http://goo.gl/7m2Uyj

19. "100 Best Companies To Work For: 2015," *Fortune.* http://goo.gl/XMq8Nt

20. Thomas C. Frolich and Douglas A. McIntyre, "American's Worst Companies To Work For," *24/7 Wall St* (June 21, 2014): http://goo.gl/h6tLBc

21. "Top Brands: Most Trustworthy," *Forbes.* http://goo.gl/WcmOna

22. Alexander E. M. Hess and Douglas A. McIntyre, "America's Most Hated Companies," *24/7 Wall St.* (January 14, 2015): http://goo.gl/BxNHDz

23. "2010 Edelman Trust Barometer Study," *Edelman* (January 22, 2010): http://goo.gl/hBFKtA

24. "5 Things You May Not Know About Bill Gates," *CNBC* (June 27, 2008): http://goo.gl/Lwxk9e

25. Emphasis added. "Company Information," *Starbucks.* http://www.starbucks.com/about-us/company-information

26. Adi Ignatius, "The HBR Interview: 'We Had To Own The Mistakes,'" *Harvard Business Review* (July 2010): https://goo.gl/15xhcz

27. Karen Freeman, Patrick Spenner, and Anna Bird, "Three Myths About What Customers Want," *Harvard Business Review* (May 23, 2010): https://goo.gl/RIo6Nk

28. "Regional Grocer Wegmans Unseats Amazon To Claim Top Corporate Reputation Ranking," *Harris Interactive* (February 4, 2015): http://goo.gl/vZurQC

29. Joyce E. A. Russell, "Career Coach: The Value Of Keeping An Eye On Ethics," *The Washington Post* (February 20, 2015): http://goo.gl/6kUeH4

30. Tony Schwartz, "The Productivity Paradox: How Sony Pictures

Gets More Out Of People By Demanding Less," *Harvard Business Review* (June 2010): https://goo.gl/VWQ5Va

31. David Segal, "Apple's Retail Army, Long On Loyalty But Short On Pay," *The New York Times* (June 23, 2012): http://goo.gl/AltLCy

32. "Company Fact Sheet," *Chick-Fil-A*. http://goo.gl/agQcE6

33. Carol Tice, "7 Fast-Food Restaurant Chains That Rake In $2M+ Per Store," *Forbes* (August 14, 2014): http://goo.gl/znixYG

34. "REI Is Closing On Black Friday," *REI*. http://optoutside.rei.com

35. Ben Harrowe, "It's Time To Blaze A New Trail Through The Black Friday Madness," *Medium* (October 27, 2015): https://goo.gl/mhQ4nX

36. Alexandra Gibbs, "REI Pays Employees To Skip Black Friday And Head Outdoors," *CNBC* (October 27, 2015): http://goo.gl/UkeWjp

37. Simon Sinek, "How Great Leaders Inspire Action," Presentation At TEDx PugetSound (September 2009): http://goo.gl/YnPbzZ

38. "Environmental Responsibility," *Apple*. http://goo.gl/aWx7rd

39. Seth Fiegerman, "Tim Cook's Philosophy At Apple, In His Own Words," *Mashable* (September 17, 2014): http://goo.gl/sED1Zy

40. Ignatius, "The HBR Interview."

41. "Zappos Family Core Value #1," *Zappos*. http://goo.gl/fHKLkN

42. Ashley Verrill, "A Zappos Lesson In Customer Service Metrics," *Customer Service Investigator* (June 7, 2012): http://goo.gl/ME4Olo

43. "ConsumerWatch: Cellphone Company Tries To Collect From

Deceased's Estate," *CBS San Francisco Bay Area* (August 17, 2012): http://goo.gl/sxZo4Z

44. Andres Jauregui, "Tina Enstad, T-Mobile Customer, Continues To Receive Charges After Death in Crash," *The Huffington Post* (October 18, 2012): http://goo.gl/oOJ7Zw

45. Jon Yates, "Problem Solver: Death In Family Results In Cellphone Charge," *Chicago Tribune* (August 12, 2012)

46. Matthew Hutson, "Quenching Consumers' Thirst for 'Authentic' Brands," *The New York Times* (December 27, 2014)

47. Andy Winkler, Ben Gitis, and Sam Batkins, "Dodd-Frank at 4: More Regulation, More Regulators, and a Sluggish Housing Market," *American Action Forum* (July 15, 2014): http://goo.gl/t3IjqR

48. Rebekah Mintzer, "3 Workplace Ethics Lessons From the Ethisphere Summit," *Corporate Counsel* (March 11, 2015): http://goo.gl/q0fil3

49. *CVS Health Code Of Conduct.* https://goo.gl/P6NzDT

50. "About DNI," *Dole.* https://goo.gl/F7jrkd

51. Jessica Wapner, "David Murdock Wants You To Live Forever," *AARP* (April/May 2013)

52. Ibid.

53. Ken Brown and Ianthe Jeanne Dugan, "Arthur Andersen's Fall From Grace Is a Sad Tale of Greed and Miscues," *The Wall Street Journal* (June 7, 2002): http://goo.gl/ALnZcZ

54. "Our Leadership Principles," *Amazon.* http://www.amazon.jobs/principles

55. John Greathouse, "5 Time-Tested Success Tips From Amazon Founder Jeff Bezos," *Forbes* (April 30, 2013): http://goo.gl/5IXquk

56. "Benchmarks By Company," *American Customer Satisfaction Index.* http://goo.gl/MXP2Vw

57. Ryan Scott, "What Motivates Employees?" *Forbes* (January 11, 2015): http://goo.gl/NGxz3W

58. Morgan Clendaniel, "The Brands That Survive Will Be The Brands That Make Life Better," *Fast Company* (November 7, 2011): http://goo.gl/qCfslM

59. Poorna Bell, "Sport England's This Girl Can Campaign Inspires Women To Get Fit By Busing Real Woman (Cellulite and All)," *The Huffington Post UK* (January 12, 2015): http://goo.gl/JK89yj

60. Maija Palmer, "Chief Executives Spread Their Wings As Fledgling Tweeters," *Financial Times* (January 28, 2015)

61. Susan Dominus, "Is Giving The Secret To Getting Ahead?" *New York Times* (March 27, 2013)

62. For more information, see Saul McLeod, "Maslow's Hierarchy Of Needs," *Simply Psychology* (2014): http://goo.gl/FOaUpv

63. Brené Brown, "The Power Of Vulnerability," Presentation At TEDx Houston (June 2010): http://goo.gl/4SZDKK

64. JetBlueCorpsComm, "Our Promise To You," *YouTube* (February 19, 2007): https://goo.gl/jRcCR0

65. Patrick Vogt, "Brands Under Attack: Marketers Can Learn From Domino's Video Disaster," *Forbes* (April 24, 2009): http://goo.gl/yqleFI

66. John Ellett, "Being Transparent To Revitalize A Brand—The Domino's Story," *Forbes* (August 25, 2011): http://goo.gl/zeuLpU

67. "Case Study: The Johnson & Johnson Tylenol Crisis," *University of Oklahoma.* http://goo.gl/llBIlp

68. Geoff Colvin, "Mary Barra's (Unexpected) Opportunity," *Fortune* (October 6, 2014)

MICHAEL WEISMAN is a 42-year veteran of the advertising and marketing industry where he guided strategic brand campaign development for some of the most iconic brands in the country by offering a panoramic view to create distinct, relevant voices in the marketplace.

In 2009, fueled by the financial and moral collapse of Wall Street, Mike Co-founded The Values Institute, a strategic think tank whose mission is to inspire values-driven corporate culture. More than a vocational pursuit, Mike views his leadership of the Values Institute as a calling. In November of 2013, in partnership with California State University Fullerton, The Values Institute formed The Center for Brand Values Communication and Research —a center of excellence designed to carry-on the work of bringing values into the boardroom and classroom by furthering values research and developing curriculum at the professional and undergraduate level.

Michael takes the story of values into boardrooms across the country where he consults with C-suite executives, and speaks to groups large and small motivating them to live a life of values both professionally and personally.

BETH JUSINO is an award-winning writer, editor, teacher, and publishing consultant with almost twenty years of experience helping storytellers and thought leaders draw out their uniquely compelling messages. She lives in Seattle.